WATER

GATE

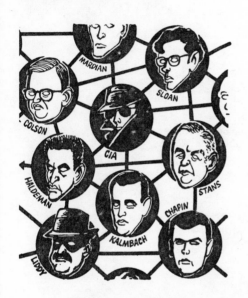

CRIME IN THE SUITES

by Michael Myerson

INTERNATIONAL PUBLISHERS New York

For Gil—with the special love one reserves for a
favorite teacher

Title page drawing by Bill Andrews
by permission of the Daily World.

©1973 by International Publishers Co. Inc.
All rights reserved
First edition 1973
Second Printing 1973

ISBN 0-7178-0410-0
Library of Congress Catalog Card Number: 73-78992
Printed in the United States of America

"Those making this plan had the same mentality employed by the Gestapo in Nazi Germany."
—Senator Sam Ervin

"The President has set out to see if you can do it in 1973 the way the Germans did it in 1933."
—Federal Communications Commissioner Nicholas Johnson

The Watergate "smacked of the situation which Hitler's intelligence chiefs found themselves in during the 1930s and 1940s."
—James McCord Jr.

"It (the White House today) is like the last days in a Berlin bunker in 1945."
—*Time* magazine

"It must be faced that the sum of all the allegations is that we were the victims of a coup d'etat or an attempted coup. I weigh my words carefully."
—Malcolm Moos, White House Administrative Assistant to President Dwight D. Eisenhower

"There are those who say that law and order are just code words for repression and bigotry. This is dangerous nonsense. Law and order are code words for goodness and decency in America.
—Richard M. Nixon
March 1973

Contents

[1]

THE COMMITTEE
TO RE-ELECT
THE PRESIDENT

IT IS early Saturday morning, June 17, 1972. Frank Wills, 24 years old, a Black $80-a-week security guard in the Watergate complex, is making his rounds. He himself lives in a one-room Washington apartment, all his meager salary can afford. The Watergate is something else again. He passes the Democratic party national headquarters and notices the lock on the door is taped. Inside men are speaking with foreign accents, crawling on the floor. They are well dressed, right down to their surgical gloves. They are equipped with walkie-talkies, a short-wave receiver set, door jimmies, lock picks, a couple of .35 mm cameras and 40 rolls of unexposed film, three pen-sized tear-gas guns, an eavesdropping apparatus, and $5,600 in new $100 bills. The Committee to Re-Elect the President (CRP) is at work.

† † †

When Wills informs the police, they hurry over to the Watergate. As they approach the

Democratic offices they have no idea that they
are literally about to open a can of worms.
Inside are four *gusanos*,[1] all CIA veterans,
and the security chief for the Republican
party. All were mercenaries together in the
invasion of Cuba at the Bay of Pigs 11 years
earlier. Across the street, at the Howard Johnson motor hotel, overseeing the operation,
was their CIA staff coordinator for the Cuban
invasion. All are political partisans of the
President of the United States, who was Vice
President and "action officer" of the invasion
of Cuba at the time plans of the invasion were
adopted. Their own former President, the
dictator Fulgencio Batista, and their adopted
President, Richard M. Nixon, had been
friends. The two leaders had been introduced
by their mutual good friend, Charles Rebozo.
At the time of arrest, the *gusanos* are performing an act of loyalty to their leaders.

† † †

Three weeks after the inauguration of the
re-elected President, another President, this
one the head of the International Brotherhood
of Teamsters, is also working in the pre-dawn
hours. Frank Fitzsimmons is visiting the
Teamster-financed La Costa country club
near San Diego, California. La Costa has been
called by a Justice Department lawyer, "the

---

[1]*Gusano* is, literally, worm, in Spanish. It is the popular
term in Cuba for those who, after the Revolution came
to power, went into exile and became active counterrevolutionaries against their former countrymen.

West Coast R and R (rest and recuperation) center for all sorts of hoods from throughout the country." Fitzsimmons is there to meet with Lou (the Tailor) Rosanova, identified by the FBI and a U. S. Senate committee investigating crime as a top Mafia figure. A few hours later, Fitzsimmons is in San Clemente where he and Richard Nixon board the Presidential jet Air Force One for a flight back to Washington.[2]

† † †

Air Force One is the site a year earlier for another important Nixon meeting. Here it is that he convinces Alabama governor George Wallace of the advisability of the southerner running in the Democratic party primaries rather than with the American Independent party. With the AIP in 1968, Wallace had garnered nine million votes which might well have gone to Nixon, who barely outpolled his major rival that year, Hubert Humphrey. The President wants a bit more security in his re-election campaign. With Wallace trying for the Democratic nomination, an obviously unrealizable goal, he would not be a factor in the November elections. The Alabaman sees the wisdom of his certain defeat when the President indicates that the government will drop its impending prosecution of Wallace's brother on tax evasion charges.[3]

† † †

[2]Los Angeles *Times*, May 31, 1973.
[3]This story was told to federal investigators by John Dean, former White House counsel.

Identical strategic considerations bring together another pre-campaign meeting in the Los Angeles Hilton in October 1971. Gathered here are Attorney General John Mitchell and White House lieutenant Jeb Stuart Magruder, who will eventually be numbers one and two at the CRP; Robert Walters, a former top Wallace aide in the AIP 1968 campaign; and a Walters assistant, Glenn Parker, now a member of the National Socialist White People's party. Mitchell argues that a poll showed that in a Nixon-Muskie race without Wallace, four-fifths of the Wallace vote will go to Nixon. The meeting concludes with a decision to give a secret cash donation of $10,000 from CRP which will be used by the Californians to hire a team of American Nazis to convince AIP voters to change their registration.[4]

† † †

Again it is after midnight, but the place is New Hampshire. Phone calls are being placed to registered Democrats, waking their families. They are irritated; these phone calls have been going on for a few days. The callers say they represent the "Harlemites for Muskie" and they ask for votes for "their" candidate "because he's done so much for Black people." The play on the racist fears of white voters is only one problem that plagues the

[4]Washington *Post*, June 7, 1973. This story was first reported in November 1972 by the *Peoples World* of Berkeley, California.

Muskie campaign. There are others. Once more it is late at night. A small-town airport. Again a phone call comes, this time to inform the field control that the Senator's plane isn't coming in after all. The controller turns off the main field lights. Moments later a plane comes down fast, without help, maneuvering to avoid disaster. Senator Edmund Muskie has narrowly escaped murder.

† † †

The offices of Hank Greenspun, editor and publisher of the Las Vegas *Sun*: Under the cover of night, a burglary is in progress. The burglars: a member of the White House staff, a CIA operative his entire adult life; and the attorney for the CRP, formerly an FBI agent. They are after hundreds of memoranda signed by billionaire Howard Hughes, dealing in part with his efforts to skirt antitrust suits with his Nevada holdings, which are valued at an estimated $250 million. The burglars are traveling using the cover of being representatives of the Hughes Tool Company. Hughes is an important contributor to the CRP, as he has been with earlier Nixon campaigns. He has supplied an airplane for the getaway; it waits nearby to take the burglars to Latin America. Flight proves unnecessary; the burglars cannot find the desired files.

† † †

Yet another top-level meeting is in progress. It is at the Justice Department in the Attorney General's office. Present are the At-

torney General, the highest legal officer in the
land; the counsel to the President, the highest
legal advisor in the White House; the temporary director of CRP, on loan from the White
House. They are listening to contingency
proposals from the CRP attorney, also on loan
to the campaign organization from the White
House staff, where he had been part of a
clandestine private police force under the
President. His suggestions at this meeting
include wiring a yacht for sound and photos,
and hiring a number of call girls to serve on
board; then inviting Democratic convention-
eers at Miami onto the yacht for purposes of
entrapment. Another proposal is to kidnap
leading members of radical groups that might
demonstrate at the Republican convention,
sequestering them in Mexico through the
period of the convention and then returning
them to the United States. The drafter of
plans is sent back to the drawing board because "the scope and size of the project"—it
would cost a million dollars—are too elabo-
rate. No legal nor moral reservations are
raised by these leaders of state.[5]

† † †

Death is in the air. An assassination team is
dispatched to Mexico enroute to kill General
Omar Torrijos, the President of Panama, because of his attempts to bring the Panama
Canal under Panamanian control. The hit
man is under $100-a-day contract to the

[5]See testimony of Jeb Stuart Magruder before Senate
Hearings on Watergate.

White House. The mission is called off inexplicably.[6]

At a meeting to plan the bugging of the Watergate the chief operations officer of the plan, who carries a gun and has the reputation as "the gun lobby's man in the Administration", threatens to kill the acting chief of CRP.[7] Both are on White House staff at the time.

✝ ✝ ✝

The CRP security chief, for over 20 years an FBI or CIA agent, and at the end of his career head of security for the CIA, had been arrested at the scene of the Watergate crime six months earlier. Now the trial is about to begin and he is balking at a deal to plead guilty so as to avoid a trial with possibly dangerous testimony, in return for which he will receive clemency from the President. He leaves his home in Maryland and goes to a public telephone booth near the Blue Fountain Inn on Route 355. He is to use the code name, "Mister Watson." Again the demand is made on him and again he hesitates. A meeting is arranged with a former member of the New York police department's Red Squad, now doing the bidding of the White House. They meet at a scenic vantage point overlooking the Potomac River and the Capitol, on the George Washington Memorial Parkway. He is

[6]Interview with John Dean, *Newsweek*, June 18, 1973.
[7]Magruder testimony *op cit.*

told, "The President's ability to govern is at stake. Another Teapot Dome scandal is possible, and the government may fall. Everybody else is on track but you. You are not following the game plan. You know that if the Administration gets its back to the wall, it will have to take steps to defend itself." The ex-FBI and CIA agent considers the meaning of this: "I took that as a personal threat, and I told him in response that I had had a good life, that my will was made out."[8]

† † †

The Pentagon Papers have been released to the press and *The New York Times* and Washington *Post* have printed portions of them, despite the Nixon Administration's attempt at prior restraint, quashed by the Supreme Court. The paramilitary White House secret police are assigned to "plug" the leak. Daniel Ellsberg has an associate, a former Kissinger aide at the National Security Council, who is now working at Brookings Institution, a D. C. think-tank. The President's special counsel sends for the White House staff gumshoe and tells him a secret police squad has to blow up Brookings to destroy some papers in its safe."[9]

† † †

On the eve of his re-election, Richard Nixon told a Washington *Star* reporter, "The

[8]See testimony of James McCord Jr. and John Caulfield before Senate Select Committee on Watergate.
[9]*Newsweek, op cit.*

average American is just like the child in the family." Now Papa Dick had organized his own *tonton macoutes*[10] The drive of the Nixon Administration to create a Presidential dictatorship is characterized by the series of crimes listed above, referred to by John Mitchell as "White House horrors." Nixon's whole career has uniquely prepared him for the role.[11] His aide John Ehrlichman has defended burglary and breaking and entering under Presidential direction as not only constitutional but part of the President's "obligation" in the interests of "national security." Asked if that constitutional obligation might include murder, Ehrlichman declined to state where the line might be drawn. The people of Indochina know that it doesn't stop at murder.

For over a quarter of a century, from Korea to Cambodia, from the jailing of Communists to the vendetta against Daniel Ellsberg, "national security" has been the last refuge of political scoundrels. The "need" for a Presidential dictatorship in the name of national security—free of legislative and judicial restraints—to make war abroad and break laws at home, was a need felt not only by Richard Nixon as an individual, but by that circle of corporation owners, military officers and in-

[10]The *tonton macoutes* were the private police force, known for their brutality, of Haiti's late President, Francois "Papa Doc" Duvalier.
[11]See the biographical sketch of Nixon, pp. 158, Roster.

telligence operatives he represents. It is a "need" that has come of a new situation in the world, where the options for the United States are more than ever limited by the growing strength of the socialist countries and the emergence of newly liberated nations; and by the growing disenchantment of our own people with their lives as they are, and their questioning of the system that cannot answer their needs. Some of the criminal activities of the White House clandestine parapolice and the CRP have come to light through the exposure of Watergate. New charges continue to roll like summer thunder.[12] In their sum they represent a desperate attempt to halt the decline of the American Empire.

[12]See the Roster for an alphabetical guide to the many Watergate conspirators, with a list of their various crimes and improprieties.

[2]

A REPORT ON
LAW AND ORDER

RONALD REAGAN, Governor of California and
a man to whose career cosmetics are no
stranger, feels that "criminal" is too harsh a
word to describe the Watergate criminals,
who are, incidentally, also his political colleagues. In a UPI interview when the case
broke open, he argued that the men "are not
criminals at heart." The governor—whose
personal vendetta against Angela Davis
caused her loss of livelihood, 18 months of
her life and came within a jury decision of
taking her life altogether—allowed as how
the Watergate conspirators were "well-
meaning individuals."

The defendants themselves agree with Reagan's estimate. Bernard Barker, for years an
officer in the secret police of Fulgencio
Batista in Cuba—a police apparatus responsible for 20,000 deaths by torture—
complained to *The New York Times* a few
months after his arrest, "It is very repulsive to
me when I read [about myself as] the 'alleged
burglar.' I think more as a cop and not as a
burglar. I'm of that formation. I have been a

19

police officer and I can't conceive of myself as a burglar." Says former Attorney General John Mitchell, under one indictment and facing several more: "I've never stolen any money. I never did anything mentally or morally wrong."[1]

With this apologia in mind, it is of value to summarize the federal statutes that have been broken, according to various grand jury and congressional testimony. Following is a partial list, with penalties that may apply if the charges are upheld in court: illegal wiretapping (five years, $10,000); knowledge of illegal wiretapping without reporting to the authorities (three years, $5,000); influencing, impeding, or obstructing the "due administration of justice," i.e. cover-ups of crimes

[1] In Bertholdt Brecht's *Three Penny Opera*, a character announces that some poor people have robbed a bank. Another character comments: "Now, that's a switch." Our point, precisely: our system—inequitable by its nature, repressive in its roots, criminal in its formation—produces its worst criminality in its leading protagonists; its direst victims come from those without power. See Chapter 3.

Further insight into Mitchell's wistful thinking came during his testimony before the Senate Watergate committee when he said he thought "in hindsight" that the White House staff should have been lined up and shot. Revealing a lack of ethics and a contempt of law that would disqualify him for the Boy Scouts much less the Justice Department, Mitchell's entire testimony rested on the premise that loyalty to Richard Nixon was more important than loyalty to the U.S. Constitution. Remarked one commentator, Mitchell was a believer in the "fuehrer principle," after the Nazi slogan, "*Ein Reich, Ein Fuehrer*" (One Country, One Leader).

(five years, $5,000); conspiracy to obstruct
justice (five years, $10,000); perjury, or lying
under oath, during a federal judicial proceed-
ing (two years, $5,000); subornation of perju-
ry, i.e. causing another person to lie under
oath (two years, $5,000); conspiracy to
suborn perjury (five years, $10,000); influenc-
ing, intimidating or impeding a witness (five
years, $5,000); interference with a campaign
for elective office (one year, $1,000); authori-
zation or distribution of unsigned or falsely
signed campaign literature (one year, $1,000);
failure of a campaign organization to report
receipts or expenditures to the General Accounting Office, and conspiracy to do same
(one year, $1,000); falsifying, concealing, or
covering up, by a government employee or
official, of material facts (five years, $10,000);
knowledge of falsification of material facts
without reporting it (three years, $5,000);
willful obstruction, delay, or prevention of
information relating to a violation of a criminal statute (five years, $5,000); income tax
evasion (five years, $10,000); theft of govern-
ment documents (ten years, $10,000); de-
struction of government documents (three
years, $10,000); false advertising (five years,
$1,000); illegal sales of firearms (five years,
$5,000); conspiracy to transport women ac-
ross state lines for purposes of prostitution
(five years, $5,000); forgery of government
papers (ten years, $1,000); corrupt attempt to
influence a federal judge (five years, $5,000);
tampering with a jury (five years, $5,000);

fraudulent use of credit cards (five years, $1,000); alteration of government records (five years, $1,000); using public office to influence private business, (two years, $10,000); tampering with the mail (five years, $2,000); bribery (fifteen years, $20,000); acceptance of bribe (fifteen years, $20,000); using government funds to bribe (fifteen years, $20,000). In addition to these federal crimes, there are several state crimes which have been committed in the course of the Watergate conspiracy. These include: illegal bank transactions, misappropriations of corporate funds, extortion, threats to murder, conspiracy to murder, conspiracy to kidnap, conspiracy to commit arson, theft, grand larceny, breaking and entering, assault and battery. These penalties are determined by the laws governing the states where they are committed.[2]

Without tongue in cheek, Richard Kleindienst announced the day after his resignation as Attorney General that "a national wave of lawlessness has been broken during the Nixon administration." In a Law Day ceremony for the District of Columbia Bar Association, Kleindienst said: "What seemed

[2]The list may not be complete, but it does cover those illegal acts that have come to public light. The reader is cautioned to remember that the penalties listed are maximum ones for *each* count. In most cases, aiding and abetting the listed crimes carries the same penalties as commission of the crimes. Conspiracy to commit any federal crime is punishable by five years and $10,000.

to be the growing popularity of lawlessness, where Americans put themselves above or outside of the law, has been halted."

It seems "the law" had a corner on the "lawlessness" market. Kleindienst and his mentor Mitchell presided over a Justice Department that produced John Dean, Robert Mardian, L. Patrick Gray, Jerris Leonard, Henry Peterson and William Sullivan. These were the top legal officers in the United States, and all were key operatives in the biggest criminal conspiracy in the political history of our country. Their Justice Department also employed Will Wilson, Mitchell's first assistant in the criminal division of the department. Wilson had been the private attorney for a man under federal investigation for fraud and from whom Wilson borrowed $30,000 after becoming chief prosecutor for the United States. Wilson has resigned.

Richard Nixon broke historical precedent and appointed a military man to the civilian post of Chief Marshall of the United States. He was Provost Marshall, General Carl Turner, who is now in prison for stealing guns from persons under arrest. It was Clarence M. Kelley, the new permanent director of the FBI, from whose custody as Kansas City police chief the guns disappeared. Elsewhere in the world of law and order, once the Watergate revelations cascaded, such principals as James McCord, John Dean and Martha Mitchell—looking over their own shoulders—told the press they feared for their lives. Dorothy Hunt was already dead in a plane crash; Congressman Mills was the first to take his own life.[3] In a demonstration of the rugged American individualism for which they had been proponents, conspirator followed conspirator—with flag pins in their lapels, the piousness of seminary students in their voices—to inform on the next conspirator in hopes of charity from the public.

By the summer of 1973, there were six grand juries across the the country, four Senate and two House hearings, all investigating separate aspects of the conspiracy. The President, who had refused to meet the press for half a year, issued regular announcements to the effect that he would not resign. While his Vice President did hold a press conference to proclaim his doubts about indictments he faces for extortion, kickbacks and tax fraud. The country had seen three Secretaries of Defense in four months, had gone more than a year without a permanent FBI director, had seen musical chairs played with top personnel at the CIA, SEC and Justice Department. After four months of the second Nixon term, 72 of the 125 White House staff members approved by the President had resigned. Of nearly 400 top level jobs in the Administration, more than half were vacant or occupied by people on the job less than four months,

---

[3] All of these names, and those not otherwise identified in the text, are listed in the Roster.

prompting one magazine to joke, "If the boss calls, get his name."[4]

If government personnel were changing quickly, their pace was exceeded by changes in the President's explanation of the affair. In September 1972, Kleindienst pledged "the most extensive, thorough and comprehensive investigation since the investigation of the Kennedy assassination." Since opinion polls have found that barely a third of the country believes the official findings of *that* investigation, the Attorney General's announcement hardly put the nation at ease. Nixon tried harder at a news conference a month later. He described the FBI's inquiries as so thorough and complete they make the 1948 Congressional investigation of Alger Hiss look "like a Sunday school picnic," another assertion not really tailored to gain the public's confidence.

Nixon's sundry rationales changed as his perimeter of defense tightened. His strategy seemed to be first to deny knowledge of any wrongdoing, then hide behind a shield of

---

[4]During the election campaign, Nixon's fund-raising operation had changed its name three times. In addition it had 450 other, separate committees throughout the states allowing large contributions to be broken down into several $3,000 donations, avoiding federal gift tax assessments. Now, while the government was virtually paralyzed, the CRP was still functioning, still collecting new millions of dollars twelve months after re-electing the President, who could not again be constitutionally re-elected.

executive privilege; then faced with accumulated evidence, to admit knowing others were
involved but simultaneously maintain their
innocence. (One satirist mimicked the President: "Everybody is innocent. However, I
accept the resignations of 1,541 of the finest
government employees I have ever known.")
Finally, as the last refuge of a cornered President, he wrapped himself in the old army
blanket of national security. In his May 1973
brief to the public, describing himself as the
author and organizer of a private police apparatus, Nixon used the phrase "national
security" 24 times, leading one to recall
George M. Cohan's observation that "many a
bum show has been saved by the flag."

The crimes exposed by Watergate had obviously created a government crisis of un-
rivaled proportions. Nixon apologists argue
that this sort of stuff goes on all the time, so
why the excitement. Of course mugging goes
on all the time too, the acceptance of which
fact hasn't exactly relaxed our urban populations. And never has the Constitution been
subject to such sustained mugging.

The growing disaffection of the poor, of
students and the young, of working people, of
the powerless of all colors, was seen as a
wave of lawlessness by the powerful, those of
"the law." So the law resorted to a true wave
of lawlessness—mass illegal arrests, assassinations, random killings of the peaceably
assembled, bag jobs of psychiatrists, forgeries
of a dead President's signature, a series of

grand juries convened to hear perjured testimony of paid government provocateurs, the burglary and buggings of newspapermen, foreign embassies, radical law firms.

A few assassinations and a decade ago, those who doubted the official story of the murder of John Kennedy were regarded as suffering from paranoid fantasies with a "conspiracy theory" of history. Now popular perceptions have changed. As the Pentagon Papers showed that a handful of men sat down and conspired against the peace of the world, the Watergate investigation shows that a handful of men sat down and conspired against our democratic liberties.

The people in their majority have begun to understand this to be the reality. For nearly a dozen years the people of the United States were told not to question government policy in Indochina, that after all the President knew best, he had all the facts, that if we knew what he knew we would be quiescent. Now in a conspiracy involving all of his closest advisors, his main financial backers, his public and private attorneys and counselors, his entire staff, much of his family and all of his dearest friends, he would have us believe he had none of the facts at all.

Popular skepticism with the government's cynicism has produced the much reported crisis of credibility. The situation reached such proportions that by 1970, in interviews in six cities, 1,700 persons said they did not accept the story that U. S. astronauts had walked on the moon. In some towns, as many as 19 percent of those interviewed did not believe in the moon walk. By early May 1973, a Louis Harris poll determined that two-thirds of those asked did not believe the White House story on the Watergate conspiracy; more alarming for the President is that only *nine percent* were willing to accept his version of the events. Perhaps such disbelief and rage will make it possible that Richard Nixon will not have the American people to kick around any more.

[3]

FOR US TO
REASON WHY

A NUMBER of explanations of Watergate have
been given by the pedants of the press. They
all are variations on one of four themes: 1)
The national soul is corroded, the weak side
of human nature has been shown, we are all
guilty; and, on the other hand: 2) The conspirators were after power, not wealth; 3)
That's politics; everybody does it; or, con-
versely: 4) The conspirators were a bunch of
rotten apples in an otherwise decent political
barrel. Each explanation has proven unsatis-
factory. In fact, most of us are not guilty, but
are victims of a conspiracy; the conspiracy
represents the greatest accumulation of private wealth in human history; that wealth is
in power and seeks to consolidate its power
to increase its wealth; in a system where
profits come first and money talks a language
well understood by all, conventional politics
is the art of the possibility to buy power, but
there are other politics that reject the conventional wisdom; in fact those conventional
politics come out of a barrel that is rotten to
the bottom. What the James Restons and Eric

29

Severeids and Stewart Alsops try to tell us is
that this is the freest of societies; that the
exposure of Watergate demonstrates the per-
fectability of the system; that, after all, in a
sense, Richard Nixon was right in his characterization of all this as only "a bizarre incident."

Nixon, Mitchell, Haldeman, and their colleagues are not abhorrent evils, political
gangsters, corrupt individuals. They may be
those, but they are more. They are heirs to
Democratic administrations as well as Republicans. They are creatures of their time
and of the political system they serve. To
understand Richard Nixon and Watergate we
must understand that time and that system.

From its inception our country has witnessed barbarism against the populace for the
purpose of private accumulation of wealth.
Black men and women were kidnapped by
the millions and brought to our eastern
shores to make cotton king of the southern
economy. They were made chattel slaves,
treated inhumanly. Since its infancy, the
United States embraced an official policy of
genocide against the indigenous peoples. To
serve the interest of the emerging cattle
barons, land developers and railroad industrialists, the Native American peoples were
driven from their homes and herded into
concentrated reservations. In the interests of
a growing capitalism, the United States ex-
tended its borders to the Pacific through the
forceful annexation of half of Mexico. Cheap

labor was imported from Asia and Europe and herded into a gruesome factory life of 16-hour workdays, to return "home" to wretched urban slums.

With the industrialization of the economy, capitalism began to search for new markets and new sources of raw materials. Reaching out to conquer new lands, the United States emerged as an imperialist power. "Manifest destiny" meant not only stretching out from sea to shining sea but overseas as well. Colonial rule was consolidated in the Philippines, Puerto Rico, and Cuba. In the journalese of the time, Latin America became "our own backyard." Still there were other imperialisms, some more powerful than ours. The first world war was fought between these empires to eliminate the weaker of the group. In that war, of course, the United States did not suffer on its own territory, a factor that allowed it to develop and grow in the next decade. But capitalism suffered its worst economic crisis in 1929 and was never able to provide a solution in peacetime. In 1940, after a decade of depression, 9.5 million American workers, 17 percent of the labor force, were still umemployed.

In those depression years, the state apparatus grew in its regulation of the economy. Private industry had proven unequal to the task of solving this crisis of capitalism. Under pressure from powerful organizations of unemployed workers, the state was forced to assume some responsibility for the welfare of its citizenry. Unemployment compensation and social security laws were passed; the government set up agencies to create jobs. With the organization of industrial unions, the government began to regulate relations between employer and employee.

Not that the state was an impartial arbiter between two equal powers. Marxists hold that all of recorded history is a history of constant struggle between those who control the wealth of society and those who produce the wealth, between master and slave, lord and serf, capitalist and worker. To the extent the state intervenes in this struggle, it is on the side that controls society. Until the Bolshevik Revolution in 1917, when workers took state power for the first time, state intervention had always been on the side of wealth, on the side of the few. Our own history is no exception. As "free enterprise" evaporated with an unequal accumulation of wealth by a few, U. S. capitalism took on the character of monopoly capitalism. By the time of the Great Depression this process was already in an advanced stage. The crisis in the economy eliminated many of the weaker enterprises and most of the weaker banks. When the state intervened in the 1930s it intervened in the interests of preserving the system of capitalism. The government became private industry's largest customer, its money borrowed from the most powerful banks, whose security the government guaranteed in return. This new and growing economic relationship is called by Marxists, state-monopoly capitalism.

The second world war enormously accelerated the growth of state-monopoly capitalism. War production became the means to end the economic crisis and provided full employment for the first time in a generation. The government apparatus grew proportionately and the convergence of government and industrial interests meshed as one. The process of monopolization was also speeded by the war. The corporate structure came increasingly under the control of a diminishing number of financial and industrial circles. In turn the state structure changed; its relationship to the increasingly monopolized (and therefore less democratic) industrial structure inevitably moved the state in a less democratic direction. Most dramatically, the tax structure changed with working people directly shouldering the burden, a third of their paychecks being taken by the government to pay the corporations for new contracts.

By the war's end the economy had radically altered. The domination of war production became a permanent feature of the economy, the one "guarantee" against renewed crisis. The war-related industries—aircraft, oil, chemical, electronics, the emerging aerospace—and the banks and insurance companies that underwrite them, came to control the economy. In turn, they came also to be the single greatest influence in the reorganized

state apparatus. The emergence of the Pentagon as the biggest sector in the bureaucracy,
and the rapid growth of the various intelligence and counterintelligence agencies during the war and the postwar period, inevitably diminished popular democratic expression.

Years later, analyzing the Watergate conspiracy, the eminent British historian Arnold
Toynbee saw its roots in the ever more concentrated government center of power, the
executive branch. This was most dangerous,
he added, because of the nature and influence
of concentrated American big business: "The
United States business is also the world's
business," writes Toynbee. "This is one of
the present facts of life, though it is a
nuisance both for United States citizens and
for the 94 percent of the planet's population
who are aliens." Moreover, U. S. business is
among the most corrupt in the world, where
the standard of ethical conduct has sunk
below the average standard in other kinds of
social relations. Toynbee sees some per-
tinence in the fact that many of Nixon's top
White House operatives came to Washington
from advertising agencies, perhaps the most
dishonest and corrupt of businesses, one
whose "business" it is to be dishonest. As if
to illustrate Toynbee's concern, an interesting
exchange took place in a grand jury appearance of former Nixon appointments secretary Dwight Chapin, one of those advertis-

ing executives. Prosecutor Seymour Glanzer was questioning the witness about Chapin's payoffs to Republican party spy Donald Segretti. "It might be," said Glanzer, "that taxpayers want to complain about him (Segretti) getting that salary doing the work he was doing." "That's none of their concern," answered Chapin. "This is private enterprise."

After the world war, a new set of political circumstances existed in the world and at home. The European and Japanese imperialisms had been severely damaged by the fighting, obviously weakening their ability to control their foreign holdings. U. S. imperialism, undamaged and with a new military potential, made its bid for world hegemony. This was to be the "American Century," said its propagandists. The snag was that the Soviet Union, even with the loss of 25 million of its people and 30,000 towns and villages, was still around and rebuilding. The Bolshevik Revolution, less than 30 years earlier, had removed for all time one-sixth of the world's land mass from foreign domination. Moreover, the Soviet Communist party's allies in China, Indochina, Bulgaria and Korea were making revolution. In eastern and central Europe, anti-fascist governments were, with Soviet help, replacing the defeated Axis allies. In Greece, Italy, France and western Europe, Communist parties had gained new prestige through their leadership of the resistance to fascism. These developments obviously had to be stopped if U. S. hegemony was to be.

With U. S. imperialism on the ascendancy, the class of corporate rulers and their political spokesmen united in a strategy of anticommunism. This meant placement of U. S. armed forces throughout the world on a permanent occupation basis, ready to fight hot wars, cold wars, "police actions," "special wars," "counter-insurgencies," "limited wars" and thermonuclear wars. With a monopoly of atomic warmaking potential, the "American Century" was assured. In the now-defunct *Colliers* magazine, U. S. political leaders and intellectuals held a round-table discussion about what to do with the Soviet Union after we had bombed and taken it over. The Central Intelligence Agency came into being and took over the intelligence services of the defeated Third Reich, theretofore the most highly skilled and knowledgeable anti-communist espionage apparatus.

Potential domestic opposition to the new strategy had to be crushed if the "American Century" was to proceed on schedule. Through the depression years, our country had witnessed its greatest upsurge of mass democratic expression. Millions of working people had been organized into industrial trade unions, despite police and vigilante violence. Similar developments occurred in cultural fields, in education and the arts. In many instances these movements were led and influenced by the Communist party. When that party initiated support for the Spanish Republic and several thousand U. S. youth volunteered to fight fascism in Spain, there were the beginnings of a mass sentiment—anti-fascism—that would come to be embraced during the second world war by our people in their overwhelming majority.

Clearly this factor had to be neutralized. The anti-communist Cold War abroad was accompanied by its domestic version, which eventually became known as McCarthyism. The FBI, local police Red Squads, Army intelligence, CIA and a dozen private snooping agencies grew enormously. Vigilante red-hunters went on the prowl. The Senate, the House, virtually every federal agency and state legislature set up their own investigative agencies to snuff out the Red Menace. Pinkeye reached epidemic proportions. Labor strikes were severely limited in the first major anti-communist legislation. The movies, schoolrooms, airwaves and churches all hid under the bed, when they were able to extract the imaginary "reds" from those enclaves. Stoolpigeons became national heros, honored with television series, White House guest dinners and filmed biographies.

It was in this climate—during the Democrat Truman's administration—that young Richard Nixon came of political age. He came into Congress for the first time calling his opponent, Representative Jerry Voorhis, "a lip-service American" fronting "for un-American

elements, wittingly or otherwise." Four years
later he defeated Congresswoman Helen
Gahagan Douglas in a race for Senate, referring to her as "the pink lady." Running for
Vice-President with Eisenhower against
Stevenson, he said the late Illinois governor "has been guilty . . . of spreading pro-
Communist propaganda." A leading member
of the House Un-American Activities Committee, he pursued State Department aide
Alger Hiss all the way to prison. The generations of the Thirties and Forties were dismissed as "twenty years of treason" by Senator Nixon, who was to serve as honorary
pallbearer for the late Joseph McCarthy. At a
staff meeting he demonstrated how to deal
with opposition. In pantomine he plunged a
knife into an imaginary opponent. "After you
get the knife in," said Nixon gleefully, "you
twist it." And he gave his wrist a twist to
illustrate what he meant. This is the man who
would today have us believe he is reborn an
innocent, a babe in the woods who can only
be faulted for, if anything, having too trusting
a nature. A child of the "American Century,"
he now presides over its conclusion in record
time.

As loyalty oaths and readiness to inform
against neighbor and co-worker became lit-
mus tests of patriotism, social movements
that rose in the 1930s and took the form of
anti-fascism during the war were stilled. As
the fear of "bolshevism" was used by Hitler

to give rise to Nazism in Germany, anti-Communism created "the time of the toad"[1] in our own country. Communists who helped organize industrial trade unions were eliminated from those unions by new laws and union officer-corporation collaboration. The Smith Act and McCarran Act outlawed the Communist party, and its leaders were sentenced to long prison terms.[2] The liberal Hubert Humphrey forced through Congress a measure setting up concentration camps. Blacklists, deportations, beatings, and expulsion from public organizations became the regular lot of thousands of Communist party members. What was aimed at Communists in the first place came at last to embrace the population at large. (The history of repression it has suffered has helped shape the Communists as the first to see embryonic fascism at work. Speaking through its General Secretary, Gus Hall, in 1970 when the Watergate

[1] *The Time of the Toad* was the name of an essay written by Dalton Trumbo in 1949. A phrase first used by Emile Zola in an exposition of the Dreyfus Affair, the time of the toad is described by Trumbo as that period "in which the nation turns upon itself in a kind of compulsive madness to deny all in its tradition that is clean, to exalt all that is vile, and to destroy any heretical minority which asserts toad meat not to be the delicacy which governmental edict declares it."

[2] The McCarran Act, passed in 1950 during the hysteria generated by the outbreak of war in Korea, was a revised version of a bill jointly proposed in 1948 by Senator Karl Mundt and Representative Richard Nixon, which Nixon himself conceded to be unconstitutional in his original formulation.

conspiracy was just taking form, the Communist party warned: "Such shifts [by monopoly capital to the Right] result from the defeats and setbacks suffered by U. S. imperialism. They are reactions to the erosion and the growing isolation of U. S. imperialism. They are expressions of support for a policy that says: 'We must fight our way out of this mess and we must clobber any opposition to this outlook at home.'")

The Watergate conspiracy has its foundations in that period of the consoldiation of state-monopoly capitalism, of the repression of democratic movements and the growth of secret police agencies in the name of anti-Communism. In 1950, Harry Truman brought the United States into war in Korea, without Congressional consent, calling those three years of carnage "a police action" and manipulating United Nations' approval after the fact. The Eisenhower-Nixon Administration picked up the French pieces in Indochina and picked up Ngo Dinh Diem from Maryknoll Seminary in New Jersey, placing him as Chief of State of the "Republic of South Vietnam" in the most outstanding of success stories of the Horatio Alger tradition.

Vice-President Nixon, an advocate of nuclear weapons against the Vietnamese, later became "action officer" in charge of plans for the invasion of Cuba. We had already "lost" China to the Chinese, the northern half of Korea to the Koreans, most of Vietnam to the Vietnamese. Now a host of bearded revolu-

tionaries had forced our man in Havana to
flee with the national treasury in his luggage.
All of the top intelligence and military plan-
ners came together, under the leadership of
the action officer, to make certain the Playa
Giron (Bay of Pigs) invasion would be the
counter-revolution to end all revolutions.

That invasion, finally conducted by the
Kennedy administration, resulted of course
in a rout, the first military defeat of U. S.
imperialism in the hemisphere's history. The
Central Intelligence Agency, which organized
the invasion, admitted defeat. A year and a
half later, President Kennedy staged the mis-
sile crisis, bringing the world to the brink of
thermonuclear incineration, the main result
of which was a promise extracted from Washington not to use armed aggression to bring
down the Cuban Revolution. A year later, the
President of the United States was assassina-
ted in Dallas. A couple dozen theories were
developed about the assassination,[3] but,

---

[3]One of the most common theories of the assassination
is that it was related to the victory of the Cuban
Revolution and eventual Kennedy acceptance of the
Revolution as an accomplished fact. Shortly before his
death, Lyndon Johnson told a top aide that he believed
the killing was part of a conspiracy. When he took
office, replacing the dead President, Johnson said he
found "we had been operating a damned Murder Inc. in
the Caribbean." A year before the assassination a
CIA-backed assassination team had been picked up in
Havana, and Johnson speculated that Dallas had been in
retaliation for this thwarted attempt. (See *Atlantic
Monthly*, July 1973.) We already know that mobster

whatever the case, only a minority of the people believed the official story of a "single crazed assassin." The FBI, CIA, Dallas police and Secret Service stumbled and restumbled over one another, "correcting" the others' and their own original versions.

The consolidation of socialism in eastern Europe and Asia, the holding at bay of U. S. forces in Korea, the Eisenhower-Khruschev "spirit of Camp David," the triumph of the Cuban Revolution, and the defeat of the "special war" in Vietnam[4] all spelled an early end

---

Meyer Lansky had a million-dollar contract out on Fidel Castro; that CIA Watergater E. Howard Hunt had urged the killing of Castro at the time of the Bay of Pigs; that syndicate leader John Roselli, a former Al Capone associate and then Las Vegas gambling don, was hired by the CIA to find someone to assassinate Fidel on the eve of the Bay of Pigs invasion; that CIA Watergater Frank Sturgis was keeper of the biggest *gusano* armaments cache, and was interviewed by federal investigators in connection with the Kennedy assassination; that Sturgis served as quartermaster of the cache in his capacity as lieutenant to Carlos Prio Socorras, Cuban president just before Batista, who brought $50 million from Cuba to Miami. In 1972 Prio and Sturgis led "Cubans for Nixon" demonstrations at the Republican Convention. Prio's office in Miami is next door to the real estate operation of Bernard Barker and Eugenio Martinez, also convicted for the Watergate crimes.

[4]The defeat of Kennedy's strategy in Vietnam is another source of speculation about the reasons for his murder. That defeat was seen most dramatically with the overthrow and assassination of Saigon dictator Diem only three weeks before Kennedy's death. Joseph Kennedy, the President's father, and a man with ties to organized crime going back to his bootlegging days during Prohi-

bition, had been instrumental in placing Diem in Saigon after the 1954 defeat of the French. The Geneva Accords that year called for a temporary military demarcation line at the 17th parallel to allow for orderly withdrawal of French forces. Afterwards, in 1956, there were to be all-Vietnam elections, internationally supervised. With the certain knowledge that Ho Chi Minh would be elected President, the U. S. rushed Diem to replace the French puppet Bao Dai. The 17th parallel was barred to mail and transportation, and the "Republic of South Vietnam" declared.

During this time a war was raging in South Vietnam between the CIA and its French counterpart, the 2eme Bureau, over influence in Indochina. Kennedy's friend and advisor, Colonel Edward Lansdale, about whom Graham Greene wrote his novel *The Quiet American*, led the CIA forces at the time. Lansdale's top aide was Col. Lucien Conein, who, as an OSS liaison with the French resistance during the second world war, had close contacts with the Corsican crime syndicate. After the war the CIA worked with the Corsican gangsters in France to try to defeat the Communist-led trade unions. The Corsicans also controlled gambling and drugs in South Vietnam at the time. Working with the Corsicans, the CIA won out over the 2eme Bureau. When Col. Conein finally retired and left Vietnam, the syndicate gave him a Corsican medal, worn as identification for secret meetings, narcotics drops, etc.

By working with the CIA in the dispute with 2eme Bureau, the Corsicans guaranteed their ability to continue the drug traffic from the Indochinese poppy fields to Marseilles and eventually into the bloodstreams of American youth. General Paul D. Harkins, Kennedy's Commander of the U. S. armed forces in Vietnam, was meanwhile supervising Air America, the CIA cargo company, to airlift Special Forces throughout Indochina, and after making the drops, to return with cargoes of opium for transport to the United States. After the deaths of Diem and Kennedy, Saigon Air Marshall Nguyen Cao Ky became President of the

Siagon regime. Ky runs the major heroin network in South Vietnam. (See *The Politics of Heroin in Southeast Asia* by Alfred W. McCoy, New York, 1972.)

One connection between the Vietnam and Cuban theories of the assassination of President Kennedy is the presence of Santo Trafficante, Jr. at a meeting in Saigon with the Corsican syndicate. Trafficante was Meyer Lansky's man in charge of Cuban narcotics during the Batista regime, and was himself an associate of Batista.

Colonel Lucien Conein's name came into the Watergate case when Nixon counsel Charles Colson testified before Senate subcommittee investigators that he had assigned E. Howard Hunt to interview Conein in connection with the Diem assassination. (The Pentagon Papers revealed that Conein was Kennedy's personal representative to the South Vietnam generals that overthrew Diem.) Hunt, hired away from the CIA by the White House to "plug" the Pentagon Papers leak had, like Conein, been with CIA in France and in contact with the 2eme Bureau and the Corsican syndicate. And of course Hunt had, under Nixon, been in charge of the *gusanos* during the Bay of Pigs invasion, and later during the Ellsberg beating at the Capitol, during the burglary of Ellsberg psychiatrist Dr. Lewis Fielding's office, and finally at Watergate.

In the Roster's biographical listings the following persons, perhaps only coincidentally, have been involved with "controlling" drug traffic under the Nixon Administration: John Caulfield, William Colby, Charles Colson, John Connolly, General Robert Cushman, John Ehrlichman, L. Patrick Gray, E. Howard Hunt, Egil Krogh, G. Gordon Liddy, Henry Peterson, William Sullivan.

Whatever the reason for Kennedy's assassination, fears emanating from that murder continue up to the present. Democratic party national chairman Robert Strauss describes Lawrence O'Brien as being very upset after the Watergate burglary. (O'Brien was Democratic party chairman at the time.) Says Strauss, "Mr. O'Brien, I think, was scared for his life. After all, he had been

to the "American Century." The unity of
agreement within monopoly capitalism, a
unity of strategy and tactics based on ascendancy to the position of world hegemony,
had now begun to crack with these important
defeats.

---

deeply involved with two assassinations (John and
Robert Kennedy) and he was just nervous."

[4]

A LONG, LONG
TRAIL AWINDING

THE SUMMER after the Kennedy assassination, Barry Goldwater captured, literally, the Republican party nomination for President. The GOP convention in San Francisco was jammed with members and supporters of the John Birch Society, White Citizens Council, Ku Klux Klan, more than a handful of American Nazis, and sundry other fascist groupings, rubbing shoulders with the "regular" Republicans to choose Goldwater as their candidate. Network newsmen inside the hall were beaten up on camera as the Republican standard bearer announced, "Extremism in the defense of liberty is no vice." In his heart, California governor Pat Brown knew Goldwater was wrong. The governor declared: "The stench of fascism is in the air." Claims that the Goldwater campaign was on the fringes of the real Republican party were laid to rest when Richard Nixon became President four years later. Among Goldwater's top campaign lieutenants were Richard Kleindienst, Frederick La Rue, Jeb Magruder, Robert Mardian and Richard Rehnquist, the first four

Watergate participants, the latter a Nixon appointee to the Supreme Court.

Air Force Reserve General Goldwater's main campaign plank was the advocacy of bombing North Vietnam and sending ground troops en masse to the South. President Johnson replied that if he were elected, not one American boy would be sent to fight in Indochina. Over two million were sent in the next four years as Johnson instituted the Goldwater foreign policy. With the Watergate revelations, not one in 10 U. S. citizens believed President Nixon's story. A nation engaged in mass murder for a decade could hardly be expected to go into shock at the news of nasty doings in high places.

Under Lyndon Johnson and Richard Nixon 1.75 million Vietnamese were exterminated, another 1.75 million permanently maimed. According to NBC news, the United States dropped more than 14 billion pounds of bombs on North and South Vietnam.[1] It is estimated that South Vietnam, with an area roughly the size of Georgia, now has 24 million craters. State Department figures say that between 1964 and 1972 more than 7.3 million South Vietnamese, one of every three inhabitants, was made a refugee by U. S. bombing. Senator Edward Kennedy's subcommittee on refugees says there are more

[1]These figures do not include Laos, where more than one-third of the people have been bombed into an underground-cave existence, or Cambodia, where U. S. bombing was at its most intensive ever.

than a quarter-million more *since* the signing of the peace treaty in January 1973. Kennedy's subcommittee also reports 826,000 war orphans and 103,000 war widows in *South* Vietnam. NBC estimates the amount of territory destroyed by chemical defoliants at 6.4 million acres. This is what President Johnson and Nixon bought with 125 billions of our tax dollars.[2]

William L. Shirer has pointed out that whereas the Germans dropped 80,000 tons of bombs on Britain in more than five years of war (and we thought it was barbaric), the U. S. dropped 100,000 tons on Indochina in the single month of November 1972, when Nixon *restricted* the bombing because peace was "at hand." Shirer, the author of *Berlin Diary* and *The Rise and Fall of the Third Reich*, is a man who knows his subject.: "Though Richard Nixon does not have the dictatorial power of Adolf Hitler—at least, not yet—he has shown in Vietnam that he has the awesome means, unrestrained by any hand, and the disposition to be just as savage in his determination to massacre and destroy the innocent people of any small nation

[2]Not all the statistics are grim: Budweiser beer announced that in the last five years of the war 47 million gallons of Bud were consumed in South Vietnam. The *Wall Street Journal* reports that the U. S. has introduced roller skating as the newest craze in Saigon. And *The New York Times* calculates that *6,250 billion* psychological warfare leaflets were dropped in Vietnam, supplying that country with necessary toilet and wrapping paper.

which refuses to bow to his dictates and which is powerless to retaliate."

† † †

It was clear to Richard Nixon, on assuming the Presidency, that just as there had been enormous changes in the balance of world forces in the past quarter-century, so had the domestic situation shifted. The question was, how to cope? During his Cinderella ride to national fame in a pumpkin shell,[3] the public had become quiescent. This was to be, in terms first coined by Henry Luce, the Silent Generation. Little wonder: tens of thousands had lost their jobs through various blacklists; hundreds more were deported; it was worth one's life to petition the government; children were followed to and from school; scientists were driven to suicide; a young Jewish couple was murdered at Sing Sing because they would not tell a lie either for Harry Truman or Dwight Eisenhower and Richard Nixon. Those were days (it is worth repeating) when the "American Century" seemed a possibility and American imperialism found a unity of views in its achievement.

By 1956 things were becoming undone. The losses abroad were accompanied by problems at home. The Black population of

[3]Nixon exploited anti-Communist pathology with FBI informer Whittaker Chambers' tale that Alger Hiss had used a pumpkin patch to hide microfilmed government secrets. A public prepared to buy Nixon was ready for anything.

Montgomery, Alabama, capital of the con-
federacy, were walking to work rather than
riding in segregation, inspired by the example of an elderly seamstress. Their leader, a
young Baptist minister named Martin Luther
King Jr., was to eventually rally the Black
masses of the United States in their majority
to active unqualified rejection of racism as a
basis of social relations. Other boycotts were
followed by sit-ins which were followed in
turn by freedom rides and demonstrations in
the hundreds of thousands. The movement
spread throughout the 50 states and it became
evident that things would never be again as
they once were. The Black liberation movement in its civil rights stage showed peoples
of other colors, including whites, that with
mass organization they could intervene in the
determination of their own destinies.

A dozen years after Montgomery, at the
height of the Indochina war, 15 million people demonstrated during the National Mori-
torium on the war. The Never Never Land of
imperialist plunder abroad, coupled with a
tranquil homefront, had evaporated. This is
the problem which faced the huge corporations that hold power, together with their
spokesmen in government: A new world situation with a changing relationship of forces,
the United States no longer able to determine
on its own what was to be, coupled with a
mass upsurge at home unprecedented in our
history. President Kennedy's chief military
strategist and Ambassador to Saigon, General

Maxwell Taylor, had written that we were in Vietnam to show to the world that wars of national liberation (Taylor described them as "so-called") would not work against a determined imperialism armed with the ultimate weapons. A decade of war culminating with the Tet offensive in 1968 by the National Liberation Front of South Vietnam proved decisively and for all time the error of Taylor's and the Pentagon's ways. The Democratic Republic of Vietnam, the southeast Asian outpost of the socialist camp, enjoyed tremendous prestige and the overwhelming support of the world's peoples in its defense against U. S. aggression. The new world situation and the mass movement at home caused the ruling class of the United States to be of more than one mind. This was the setting for the ascendancy of Richard Nixon to the Presidency in 1968.

† † †

There is no way to look at Watergate without seeing Vietnam. The same men, the same system, the same agencies, the same ideology, the same interests that caused the slaughter of the innocents of Indochina brought about the Watergate conspiracy. And they told the same lies. Jerry Friedheim, the Pentagon's Ron Ziegler, denied reports of U. S. bombing of the Bach Mai childrens' hospital in Hanoi *after* millions of Americans had seen the devastation on network television news programs; and after General Telford Taylor had cabled *The New York Times* his eyewitness report. A week later Friedheim was forced to admit that "some limited accidental damage" had occurred at the hospital, leveled to the ground, but he suggested it was caused by "North Vietnamese ordnance or aircraft." That week, while the United States was terrorizing civilian Hanoi populations with carpet bombings, Friedheim warned that if North Vietnamese prison camps were hit, wounding U. S. POWs, Hanoi would be held responsible "under the Geneva Convention." This sort of madness earned Friedheim the Defense Department Medal for Distinguished Public Service a week later. The Pentagon citation read: "He has provided with faultless professionalism clear, concise, accurate and timely information concerning the worldwide activities of the Department of Defense."

This twilight zone of Nixonian language reached its apex with the President's evoking "national security" to account for burglaries and $10 million in home repairs. Yet to be accounted for are the hundreds of wardrooms for paraplegic vets, the napalmed corpses, the tens of thousands of teenagers driven to prostitution to service the local air bases, the army of junkies living not-so-quiet lives of desperation, the bodies in rubber bags at peace with honor.

James McCord and Jeb Magruder in their testimony to the Ervin committee, and Richard Nixon in his brief to the nation explaining why he set into motion an illegal private White House police force, all describe their acts as countering a nation in insurrection. "Thousands of campus riots," said McCord, although the evidence shows that virtually every campus demonstration against the war was non-violent. The exceptions showed the work of government *provocateurs*; when violence came it was through the barrels of police and national guard rifles—at Orangeburg, Augusta, Jackson State, Texas Southern, Louisiana Southern—and the violated, the dead, were students. Usually Black students.

At Kent State, the day of the U. S. invasion of Cambodia, Allison Krause placed a flower in a National Guardsman's rifle barrel and said softly, "Flowers are better than bullets." The next day, she and three fellow students lay dead, answered by the government. Richard Nixon had called the invasion of Cambodia an act "to protect our men who are in Vietnam and to guarantee the success of our withdrawal and Vietnamization program." He called Allison and her friends "bums." Soon after the killings the governor of Ohio convened a state grand jury; its report was so crude and transparently fallacious, a federal judge ordered it "physically destroyed." The FBI found, in its report, that there was "some reason to believe that the claim by the National Guard that their lives were endangered by the students was fabricated subsequent to the event." That was mysteriously ordered placed "under lock and key" for 75 years. The President's own appointed "Commission on Campus Unrest"

under former Pennsylvania governor William
Scranton, concluded that "indiscriminate fir-
ing of rifles into a crowd of students and the
deaths that followed were unnecessary, un-
warranted and inexcusable." The President
ignored his own commission's findings. In
late spring 1973, at the height of the Watergate revelations, a petition bearing 50,000
signatures of Kent State students and friends
was presented to the White House by Dean
Kahler, a student who lost use of both his legs
as a result of the shootings. The petition
called for a federal grand jury to investigate
the Kent State murders. A similar petition
had two years earlier been presented to then
Attorney General John Mitchell to no avail.
This new petition met a similar fate; this time
at the hands of new Presidential counsel
Leonard Garment.[4] In the first Nixon term
over 20 grand juries were convened to hand
down indictments against antiwar activists—the Vietnam Veterans, Chicago 8, the
Berrigans, Daniel Ellsberg, etc.

Former Presidential counsel John Dean
told the Ervin committee that Nixon was
frenzied over "even the smallest demonstrations" against his Vietnam policies.[5] The

[4]In July 1973, the Justice Department announced new
inquires into the Kent State murders, stimulated by the
revelations that an FBI informer, now a member of
the District of Columbia police force, may have fired the
shots which killed the first student.
[5]According to one observer, the Senate hearing room
during this testimony "was so quiet you could hear a
guillotine drop."

White House was obsessed with opposition
and chief of staff H. R. Haldeman ordered that
"any means—legal or illegal"—be taken to
eliminate protest. One day, Dean relates,
Nixon "happened to look out the windows of
the residence of the White House and saw a
lone man with a large 10-foot sign stretched
out in front of Lafayette Park." Haldeman
gave the order that "the sign had to come
down." Appointments secretary Chapin said
that "he was going to get some 'thugs' to
remove that man from Lafayette Park."

If the White House was prepared to hire
thugs to eliminate a lone demonstrator, to
what lengths were they prepared to go when
the Pentagon Papers were released? Answer:
to *any* lengths. Daniel Ellsberg's telephone (it
was brought out in his trial) was illegally
tapped even before he released the papers.
After the leak came more taps, of his phone
and those of colleagues in the White House
and the National Security Council; White
House counsel Charles Colson advocated
firebombing the Brookings Institute; the CIA
put together a psychological profile on Ellsberg, the first such CIA profile of a U. S.
citizen; a team of Cuban exiles, former CIA
agents, was organized to physically beat Ellsberg on the steps of the Capitol building; the
office of his psychiatrist was burglarized; he
was brought to trial for espionage and top
White House aides gave perjured testimony
for the prosecution; the judge was invited to
meet with Nixon at the San Clemente White

House during the trial, where Nixon asked the judge to consider the FBI directorship.

The real importance of the Pentagon Papers is that they show a 25-year history of lies and deception, war crimes and crimes against the peace, calculated on a daily basis by five successive administrations. They are the People's case in a new Nuremburg trial of U. S. war criminals. Their publication by *The New York Times* and *Washington Post* came after weeks of internal debate at those newspapers and signified the high point of opposition to the Indochina war from within the ruling class. That opposition from on high came with the realization of a war that was unwinnable (as shown most dramatically during Tet 1968), and which had caused disaffection among three-quarters of the population. The question was shifting from how to run southeast Asia to how to run the United States.

Nixon opted for burglaries and beatings, bribery and buggings—for the Watergate conspiracy. It was with the release of the Pentagon Papers that the "plumbers unit" was formed and G. Gordon Liddy and E. Howard Hunt brought into the White House to operate the Presidential secret police. Among the homes and offices illegally tapped or burglarized by the White House were those of at least a dozen newspapermen and columnists, the NAACP Legal Defense Fund, the Chilean Embassy and the homes of three Chilean diplomats, Texas Democratic party leader Robert Strauss, Michael Lerner and others of the Seattle 7, Black Panther and Weatherman attorney Gerald Lefcourt, the Harrisburg "conspiracy" defendants, Detroit 13, Vietnam Veterans attorney Carol Scott, the Communist party, Brookings and of course the Democratic party offices at Watergate. Mail sent to George McGovern and Edmund Muskie was held up and opened at the D. C. post office. The plumbers unit was hardly breaking new ground. Army Intelligence officers and the FBI had broken into the office of the *Washington Free Press*, an antiwar paper, on the eve of Nixon's *first* inauguration. An FBI official admitted that "We've been doing burglaries for years. We did them regularly, as a matter of policy."[6] There had been room at the tap throughout the Cold War, but now the taproom was in the White House basement.

Coordinating its affairs with the Justice Department, the White House ordered *agents provocateurs* into antiwar organizations to entrap people who believed all the good things engraved on those white marble buildings in the capital. In Camden, New Jersey, the FBI provocateur and chief witness against 28 pacifists who destroyed draft files, testified that the 28 had actually cancelled their plans to destroy the files. But, admitted the

[6] After J. Edgar Hoover's death it was revealed that he had a special vendetta against the Rev. Martin Luther King Jr. Wiretaps, attempted extortion and threats were used to bring Reverend King to heel. The attempts were of course unsuccessful, but the revelations have renewed calls for a reinvestigation of his assassination.

agent, "I provided the aid and strategy they needed to get into the building. This raid would not have happened without me and the FBI," all on instructions of "someone in the little White House in California." It was a set pattern, established in a score of trials—provocation, entrapment, a grand jury investigation with perjured testimony, indictments on "conspiracy" charges and long, expensive trials.

One of the most effective antiwar demonstrations took place at the end of April 1971, and culminated on May Day in the illegal arrest, by Attorney General Mitchell and his deputy Kleindienst, of 14,500 peaceful demonstrators. The week started with an encampment of several hundred Vietnam veterans in the shadow of the Capitol building. The well-disciplined, fatigue-clad Vietnam Veterans Against the War (VVAW) marched past the steps of Congress and threw away the medals they accumulated for their years of combat. President Nixon was so concerned about the potential effect of the demonstration that he demanded hourly reports "in the minutest detail," according to John Dean. The impact was profound on a nation which rates the man in uniform of his country several pegs above the fireman who rescues a child's kitten from the neighbor's tree. The White House sought to put a quick stop to the "Dewey Canyon III" encampment. Several hundred thousand other Vietnam vets with memories of the barbarism, now at home with unemployment rates equal to the worst of the depression, might themselves be moved to action. The VVAW had trouble getting a park permit; and once granted, it was not enforced, leading the federal judge to call Assistant Attorney General L. Patrick Gray on the carpet for his disrespect of the law.

White House counsel Charles Colson[7] quickly organized an ersatz pro-Nixon "Vietnam Veterans for a Just Peace" in an attempt to neutralize the effect of the VVAW. Colson's veterans' group was headed by Mel Stevens, a Navy vet working for Colson in the White House. When John Kerry, the most articulate VVAW spokesman at Dewey Canyon III, announced his candidacy for office in Massachusetts' Fifth District, Colson took it upon himself to defeat Kerry. The district is also Colson's home district. One of Kerry's opponents was Roger P. Durkin, the Conservative candidate, whose stock firm was facing an SEC investigation for a series of illegal acts performed while losing $200,000 in four years. Colson, whose father is the SEC attorney in Boston, and who himself claims credit for the appointment of then SEC chairman G. Bradford Cook, arranged to have the investigation of Durkin dropped in exchange for Durkin dropping out of the race and throwing his votes to John Kerry's Republican opponent. Colson's law partner, Charles

[7]See Colson's profile, the Roster. The paymaster for Liddy and Hunt, he is by most accounts the organizer of Nixon's private police.

Morin, emceed a fundraising testimonial for
the Republican candidate, Paul Cronin, at
which Spiro Agnew was the featured speaker.

The vengence harbored for the VVAW by
Richard Nixon reached a peak with the indictment of eight VVAW members and supporters in Gainesville, Florida, in 1972. Again
the pattern held to form—a grand jury indictment based on perjured testimony by FBI
infiltrators and provocateurs. The government agents in this case included several CIA
gusanos, some with close ties to the White
House secret police unit which bugged the
Watergate. The charge against the vets was
"conspiracy," this time to use violence to
disrupt the Republican convention—another
Reichstag fire to justify the Watergate conspiracy. The frame-up was organized by Mike
Carr, a CRP organizer in Florida and an aide
to Republican Senator Edward Gurney, Nixon's foremost apologist on the Senate's
Watergate committee.[8]

† † †

[8]As the Gainesville trial opened, in July 1973, FBI
agents were found tapping the phones in the room next
to the defense attorneys' office. The two key prosecution witnesses include a former local cop, who con-
tradicted his own testimony several times; and an FBI
infiltrator with a history of psychiatric disability. As in
the Ellsberg case, the prosecution witheld from the
defense vital trial documents, in violation of the
Supreme Court's famous "Jencks Decision." Once again
the government met defeat in its conspiracy as the
veterans were acquitted on all counts.

The VVAW was not the only group of Vietnam vets which received White House attention. Nixon's top domestic aide John Ehrlichman arranged interviews with veterans of the My Lai massacre to put together a story contradicting newspaper accounts of the slaughter. The murders of 347 old men, women and children had occurred at the end of Lyndon Johnson's term but did not come to public light until halfway through Nixon's first four years. Twenty-six officers and men were charged with murder or lesser crimes, followed by 25 acquittals and dismissals. The lone guilty verdict was returned against Lt. William L. Calley, Jr., who became an object of special Nixon concern; the President announced that he would render the final verdict on Calley. Appealing Calley's conviction, his attorneys argue that Calley "possessed no malice at all on the date of the *alleged* incident" (the incredulous emphasis mine—M.M.). The appeal is based on the thesis that in a guerilla war the burden is on the villagers to demonstrate that they are not combatants. Calley is compared to a doctor performing euthanasia; he had "considered the people killed only as enemy to be wasted," a sentiment bound to find a sympathetic ear in Commander-in-Chief Nixon.

The Nixon Administration and the powerful forces it represents came to believe that, faced with an impending defeat of imperialist goals in Indochina, its options were becom-

ing increasingly limited. Popular democratic
opposition would narrow those options still
more; hence channels of opposition expression must be shut off. The National Guard
against students and ghetto dwellers would
not alone suffice; nor would beatings and
"conspiracy" trials of radical dissenters be
sufficient. The ruling class itself was sharply
divided because of the mass disaffection, and
those opposition forces within it had also to
be silenced. A campaign was launched to
discredit network television news and the
metropolitan press; Congress was encouraged
towards self-immolation; and, finally, the
Presidential elections of 1972 were manipulated and sabotaged beyond recognition as
"free choice," even by Cook County standards.

After the re-election and the signing of the
Vietnam peace treaty, the spirit of Watergate
still prevails. The manufactured pro-Nixon
advertisements; the forged telegrams of support for the President's Vietnam policies in
an attempt to distort public opinion polls; the
paid demonstrations to counter opposition
protests; the setting up of bogus veterans
groups to neutralize the real thing; the erosion of the constitutional powers of congress
and the prerogatives of the press—in sum, the
drive toward a Presidential dictatorship to
centralize political power in the White
House—did not end with the U. S. defeat in
Vietnam. On the contrary, Nixon claims of

"peace with honor" to the contrary notwithstanding, the loss of Vietnam increased the desperation of those that control our country. "Peace with honor" is used to turn defeat into victory, just as for years the most intense warmaking in history was called "winning the peace." The first military defeat sustained by the United States armed forces—seen by the world's peoples as most striking evidence of a shift in the world balance of forces—had to be seen by our own people as "peace with honor" if their basic allegiance to the prevailing system were to hold firm.

The return of U. S. pilots from Vietnamese prisons allowed the Nixon administration to jingoistically rally the population to the idea of peace with honor. No matter that 55,000 other soldiers had returned home in body bags, some with smuggled heroin concealed in their flesh; nor that 100,000 others returned with needles in their arms, if they still had arms; nor that unemployment among veterans was thrice that of the population as a whole, itself suffering from the highest unemployment rate in a generation; nor that the government's compassion for the returning prisoners did not extend to their millions of comrades in arms: the new Nixon budget eliminated a billion dollars for public employment, affecting mainly veterans; fiscal cuts on V. A. hospitals closed down the equivalent of 17 hospitals for veterans; Administration opposition defeated congressional motions for drug rehabilitation and job placement services for the most desperate vets.

No matter: the POWs were marching home to an orchestrated chorus of an adoring press. Like instant replays, every day for a month we were treated to the same scene: mercenary officers in dress uniforms stepping off the plane, first in the Philippines, then in Hawaii, next in California, finally in their home towns, to pronounce God's blessings on the Commander-in-Chief. In Honolulu, a red carpet was literally spread for them; flags at half-mast in mourning for Presidents Truman and Johnson were hoisted to full staff; the nation's biggest employers offered public relations jobs to those who chose to leave the service; a lifetime pass to all major and minor league baseball games was offered by baseball commissioner Bowie Kuhn; all POWs were given a new Ford for a year without cost; the Orlando, Florida, Chamber of Commerce gave an all-expenses-paid week's vacation in Orlando—including admission to Disney World and other spots—to returning prisoners and their families.

The rewards were returned with new thanks for the President at precisely the moment he was in trouble with runaway food prices, ITT subversion in Chile and the Watergate investigation. The POWs' enthusiasm for the man who caused their predicament in the first place should have come as no surprise. After all, these were officers for the most part, mercenary soldiers, the most professional of killers. For insurance, a hundred military P.R. men were assembled in Hanoi and the Philippines to orchestrate the return home. Newsmen were barred from Hanoi and Saigon to interview or even silently observe the release of the pilots. At Clark Air Base the released prisoners were kept in isolation for several days; first interviews were granted only to two senior prison camp leaders who were carefully briefed beforehand by information officers. When some prisoners were allowed to talk to the press they were accompanied by Pentagon brass who ruled out "controversial" questions. Prisoners who wished to speak with their hometown press were barred from doing so but were allowed to accept written questions and counseled on which ones to answer. The result was a series of televised ceremonies with each on-camera officer appearing to have been turned on the same lathe as the one previous. The program, originally called Operation Egress Recap by the Pentagon, now called Operation Homecoming, was prepared by the Navy's neuropsychiatric research center in Point Loma, California. Under the guise of protecting the prisoners' stability, the Clockwork Orange project allows the Defense Department to keep the prisoners under strict control. For the next five years, the more than 500 officers will be on "convalescent leave" from military hospitals,[9] subject to recall at any time. We are assured of their presence at each of Richard Nixon's next several crises.

On the day of Congressman William Mills' suicide upon being implicated in Watergate, and Jeb Magruder's agreement to turn states' evidence, and Bernard Barker's description of the burglary of Dr. Fielding's office in Beverly Hills, and CIA refutations of Nixon claims in his public brief on Watergate, and L. Patrick Gray's announcement of having discussed the Watergate cover-up with the President two weeks after the burglary—on that same day, Richard Nixon assembled the former prisoners in Washington to receive *their* assurances anyway that he was still Commander-in-chief. To standing applause he said, "It's time to quit making heroes out of those who steal secrets and publish them in the newspapers." But he brought down the house when he proposed a champagne toast

[9]The POWs, in the words of one reporter, "looked a lot healthier than most of the people in the South Bronx. They are, in fact, the healthiest looking crowd of prisoners of war in history." Television viewers witnessed the grim sight of Vietnamese men and women without eyes, with warped limbs or no limbs at all, being released from Saigon's prisons in exchange for our POWs, cruel evidence of the contrasting treatment accorded prisoners by the Saigon regime.

The week the Ervin Senate committee hearings on Watergate began, Reuters reported that Col. Nguyen Van Ve, replaced in 1971 as director of South Vietnam's Con Son Island prison, after the "tiger-cage" punishment cells were revealed, had been reappointed to his old post.

to those who carpet-bombed civilian populations in Hanoi the previous Christmas.

† † †

When Watergate conspirator Jeb Magruder testified before the Ervin committee, he argued that the crimes of the White House and CRP were committed to counter "crimes" of the peace movement, although Magruder allowed that "two wrongs don't make a right." The antiwar "crime" he cited was the burning of draft cards. While Magruder and his superiors in the White House were plotting their burglaries, forgeries, briberies and beatings in secret, and denying their conspiracy upon being found out, the peace movement was meeting in open concert for all the world to see and judge, prepared to accept the consequences of its acts. The distinction between criminal and civil disobedience is perhaps too subtle for a government without scruples to ascertain.

More grotesque is the fact that the "draft-card burners" were matched against a government making war against a peasant people, in violation of the U. S. Constitution, all international law, the Geneva Accords of 1954 and the United Nations Declaration of Human Rights. Burning draft cards is compared to burning babies to death, and in defense of the latter a Presidential election was fixed, although "two wrongs don't make a right." There must have been clerks like Magruder—hair trimmed neat as the pin of the flag in his lapel—presiding over places like Buchenwald.

Even while Magruder was talking, U. S. air force bombers were bombing Cambodia at the rate of 50,000 tons a month.[10] This is one and a half times the intensity of the Christmas bombings of Hanoi, when we were dropping the equivalent of a Hiroshima-type bomb every other day. Nearly half of Cambodia's seven million people have been made refugees by the carnage. Even while the Watergate crimes were coming to light, it was revealed that Nixon had approved over 3,600 secret bombings (100,000 tons) of Cambodia in 1969-70, then ordered the Pentagon to falsify its own records to keep the bombings secret from Congress and the people of the United States, all this while Secretary of State William Rogers told the Senate: "Cambodia is one country where we can say with complete assurance that our hands are clean and our hearts are pure." The destruction visited

---

[10]Lest one think that Indochina is an aberration to an otherwise just foriegn policy, one should keep in mind the various Watergate relationships to, say, Latin America: the planned assassinations of Cuban and Panamanian premieres, Castro and Torrijos; burglaries of the Chilean embassy and homes of Chilean diplomats; ITT-CIA attempts to fix elections in Chile and overthrow the Popular Unity government; covert operations in Mexico; Vesco, Hughes, Rebozo, Abplanalp, Hunt, and Barker financial operations in Costa Rica, the Bahamas, Nicaragua, and elsewhere; the shift of organized crime's Caribbean base from Cuba to the Bahamas, with the help of Nixon associates and *gusanos*.

upon Cambodia is carried out without legal pretext, without "withdrawing troops to protect," without a treaty with the Cambodian government. A basic principle understood by any high school civics class is that killing outside of the law is murder. But the President and his Attorney General said that the murder would continue even though Congress, the legal body for war-making, demanded it stop. One is led to speculate that, even though Congress has succeeded in cutting off public monies for bombing Cambodia, the President will ask the CRP and his personal friends for help. They appear to have unlimited funds and are not, after all, above illegal activities.

Premier Pham Van Dong told a delegation visiting Hanoi in May 1973: "It is true that they [the United States] have done a great deal of damage and caused heavy losses, but we will recover. The United States, however, has suffered defeats that can never be erased." Not least among the defeats are those rendered our sensibilities.

[5]

CRIME IN THE SUITES

THE BUYING of the President 1972 in large part consisted of fundraisers Maurice Stans and Herbert Kalmbach using extortion tactics on corporations in disputes over cost overruns[1] on federal contracts, income tax cases, and disputes with the Securities and Exchange Commission. The ITT, Vesco, Litton, and dairy trust cases have received a good deal of public exposure but they are only loose threads in a fabric cut from the system of state-monopoly capitalism. For example, Richard Mellon Scaife of Gulf Oil gave CRP a million dollars; J. Paul Getty of Getty Oil contributed $100,000; Chicago insurance tycoon Clement Stone, seven million dollars between 1968 and 1972. Arthur Watson of IBM added over $300,000; Leonard Firestone

---

[1]Corporations with government contracts, particularly those engaged in war production, present Congress with one estimate of production costs to get approval with a minimum of popular opposition. Once the contract is signed and production underway, the contractors "discover" new production costs, milking the public for new monies on the rationale that the original outlay will be wasted if production is not completed.

of Firestone Rubber, $100,000; the Associated Milk Producers, $782,000; National General Corporation, a quarter of a million dollars. These were not blackmailed donations, nor were they offerings of believers to a church in which they kept faith. Rather they were down payments on goods to be received.

Northeastern railroads were allowed to reorganize exempt from antitrust laws and environmental regulations. The Peabody Coal Company was given approval for unregulated strip-mining without regard for ecological considerations. The Penn-Central railroad had already been operating on government subsidies; the welfare program for the monopoly would now continue. H. Ross Perot, Texas millionaire and financier of much of the "POW-MIA" pro-Nixon propaganda, received several government contracts for his Electronic Data Systems, Inc., which is now under congressional investigation. James R. Smith went from a position as Washington lobbyist for the utilities interests to the post of Assistant Secretary of the Interior for Water and Power; Pinckney Walter, a consultant to the natural gas companies, and Russ Moody, a lawyer for Texas oil interests, were named to the Federal Power Commission. It seemed a fair exchange: Lawrence J. O'Connor Jr. left the commission to become vice president for Standard Oil of Ohio; and Carl Bagge left his commission job to become president of the National Coal Association. Phillips Petroleum sent Robert Bowen to the Treasury

Department office which deals with oil and energy, and Tenneco's Ed Bridges went to the Commerce Department to work on East-West trade deals. Examples abound, but these few will suffice to describe the intertwining of the state apparatus and capitalism in its highest stage.

A common practice to Democratic and Republican Administrations alike—the appointment of Ambassadors based on political favors—continued under Nixon, with inflation bringing even more dollars. Henry Catto was named Ambassador to El Salvador for a $25,000 CRP donation; Anthony Marshall gave $48,000 to become envoy to Trinidad and Tobago; it cost John Humes $100,000 to occupy the U. S. Embassy in Austria; Vincent P. de Roulet and family paid $115,000 to be Nixon's rep in Jamaica (he was later kicked out for insulting that government); Ruth Lewis Farkas is now Ambassador to Luxembourg, the result of her $300,000 contribution. IBM's Arthur Watson, Nixon's first-term Ambassador to France, gave $300,000; his brother-in-law, John Irwin, gave $50,000 and replaced Watson for Nixon's second term. Walter Annenberg remains Ambassador to England for $254,000.

Litton Industries, the California-based conglomerate, produced Roy Ash, a financial angel for Nixon and his new director of the Office of Management and Budget. Litton is being paid $5 million in taxes each week to build the long-delayed LHA amphibious-assault ships. Nine ships were originally contracted for at the cost of $1 billion, but cost overruns will give the government only five ships at the same cost.

The Grumman Aerospace Corporation, another source of Nixon funds, contracted to produce 313 F-14 interceptor planes for the Navy. The contract price was $16.8 million per plane, but once production started, Grumman also reported price overruns, saying it would need $2.4 million more for each plane in order to make a "reasonable profit." The Navy said it couldn't afford the extra cost, but Gen. Robert F. Cushman Jr., the Marine Corps Commandant, former CIA director and Nixon crony, said the Marines would split the cost so Grumman could continue.[2]

In 1969, early on in Nixon's first term, A. Ernest Fitzgerald, a top Air Force price analyst, disclosed to Congress that there would be a $2 billion cost overrun in production of the C-5A transport plane. Nixon immediately dismissed Fitzgerald from his job. The President and the Air Force said the analyst was dropped as "an economy move."

With the U. S. armed forces removed from Vietnam, and with the arms limitations agreements with the Soviet Union, logic would argue that large cuts in the military budget would be impending. But corporate

[2]Grumman's legal problems are handled by Charles Colson's law firm. See the Roster for more on Cushman and Colson.

logic works only in the direction of a higher
rate of profit. Hence the second Nixon Administration is adding $5 billion of military
spending to that of 1972, while cutting $4.2
billion in social programs, leading one big-
city mayor to call the approach, "the Vietnamization of our urban problems." The
characterization is apt. What wealth corporate power was unable to accumulate in
Indochina, it will make up for in the United
States.

Even the poverty program, on its way to the
cemetery in the custody of mortician Nixon,
is seen in its last moments as a possible
source of corporate profits. At a Georgetown
cocktail party, Office of Economic Opportunity (OEO) chief Howard Phillips reported that
36 community development corporations receiving government support would be com-
pletely reorganized to reflect a "business ori-
entation," and would be transferred from
Health, Education and Welfare to the authority of the Commerce Department. The OEO
report emphasized that the corporations' activities should shift from community development to "economic development," a
euphemism for ghetto capitalism. The report
was drafted by an OEO task force under the
chairmanship of William S. P. Cotter, who is,
as vice president of Smith, Barney and Company, a New York investment and banking
firm, an "authority" on the problems of the
poor.

In Richard Nixon's new tax structure, federal taxes on wages are increasing $20 billion per annum, but corporate taxes are being cut by $25 billion. Thus, in the first quarter-year of Nixon's second term, Standard Oil of California's profits rose 24 percent. Other corporations had similar good fortune: Standard Oil of Indiana, up 21 percent; Shell Oil, up 49 percent; Atlantic-Richfield, up 52 percent; Exxon, up 43 percent; Xerox, up 22 percent; General Motors, up 26 percent; Kennecott, up 16 percent; Alcoa, up 19 percent; ITT, up 45 percent; AT&T, up 22 percent; Sperry Rand, up 46 percent; A & P, up 25 percent. On the other hand, the 1973 wholesale price index will rise 25 percent over that of 1972. Housewives, consumers and working people are now paying back tenfold the big contributions to the CRP. A & P's profits are up by a quarter because its prices on meat, poultry and fish are also up 25 percent. Meanwhile, wages remain frozen. The Committee to Re-Elect the President is one campaign organization that makes good on its promises.

† † †

The Nixon Administration and the huge corporations for whom it speaks have decided to make up for what they cannot win abroad by trying to take it at home from the working people and the poor of our own country, especially the Black and Brown people. To concentrate now on extracting maximum profits from U. S. working people means they must try to eliminate avenues of democratic protest, a pattern established in imperialism's client states. An increasing racism is used as a corporation tool to save $25 billion a year in wage differentials between white and Black workers, and to divide potentially united opposition against itself. Those who do not accept their assigned places in Richard Nixon's "new majority" can expect, at the least, vilification. Those who organize to resist illegitimate authority and move for a fundamental reordering of power in our society will be painted with a criminal face, as the blame for society's crises is placed on its victims rather than its perpetrators.[3]

Howard Phillips, a former leader of the right-wing Young Americans for Freedom, was dismissed as acting director of OEO in June 1973 after illegally serving for several months without Congressional confirmation. That was the least of his illegalities. Among other things, he turned the poverty agency "into a miniature FBI to spy on the poor."[4]

---

[3]President Woodrow Wilson once wrote: "The masters of the government of the United States are the combined capitalists and manufacturers of the United States. . . .Policy in this country comes from one source, not from many sources. . . .The men really consulted are the men who have the biggest stake—the big bankers, the big manufacturers, the big masters of commerce, the heads of railroad corporations and of steamship lines." Wilson, a man who knew whereof he spoke, would undoubtedly add military industrialists to an updated list.

[4]The words are those of columnist Jack Anderson, as is the research for this paragraph.

CRIME IN THE SUITES

Chief OEO inspector is Eric Biddle, an ex-CIA agent, who oversees the two dozen inspectors. Among his operatives are: Ray McConnon, a former CIA intelligence analyst, and an investigator for the House Internal Security Committee, the former HUAC; Peter Spalding, previously an Army intelligence officer involved in planning and coordination of investigations with the CIA and FBI; Early Morgan, formerly a government supervisor "in the fields of counterespionage, counter-subversion, and personnel security investigations," and later an Army counterintelligence agent; Gerald Crawford, for 20 years in Army intelligence handling "sensitive classified operations"; Rene Francazi, also a 20-year man in Army intelligence, retiring at the rank of colonel; Thomas Fitzpatrick, former director of San Francisco's police Red Squad; and Robert Lidenbrandt, formerly chief deputy sheriff in charge of investigations in Modoc County, California.

The "war on poverty" has become a war on the poor. Federally-funded public housing, subsidized rent and Model Cities programs are being eliminated on the rationale that "the government does not want to be a slum lord." Government manipulations in the name of "making communities self-sustaining" are eliminating all migrant health programs, neighborhood health centers, family health centers and about half the community mental health centers in the country. These include lead poisoning and rat control

programs. Not one penny is being allocated
for hospital construction, and medical research is being severed from federal funding,
save for the areas of cancer and heart disease.
Job programs in depressed areas, school construction, student loans and public libraries
are also eliminated from the federal budget.

Overt political suppression of spokesper-
sons and organizations seeking change is a
regular occurrence in every region of the
country. Especially severe is the repression in
the South as the powers that be seek to maintain the centuries-old white supremacy. Sam
Ervin's native North Carolina, the center of
the "enlightened New South" and the most
affluent state in the Old South,[5] has become a
laboratory for new methods of racist repression. Leaders of the Black liberation movement are victims of a systematic plan which
has placed dozens of their numbers in prison
for terms stretching from 20 to 80 years. A
federal judge in the state has said in court
that what is needed now is "several Lieutenant Calleys" to eliminate the "trouble-
makers." A relatively new vigilante group
calling itself "The Rights of White People"
has outflanked the Ku Klux Klan, branding
the latter group "too moderate," as it patrols

[5]"Only" 11.1 percent of North Carolina's white families
live under the poverty level; figures for Black families
total 38.7 percent. In Arkansas, by comparison, the
respective percentages are 17.7 and 52.7; in Mississippi, 15.9 and 59.2. (Source: U. S. Census Bureau.)

the streets of North Carolina with machine
guns. Bombings against the Black communities are a nightly occurrence in some towns,
but state police conduct stop-and-frisk
searches along the highways, looking not for
the bombers but for their intended victims.

Native Americans, averaging a *gross* annual
income of $1,500, an infant mortality rate
three times that of whites and a suicide rate
20 times as high as whites, have again organized themselves to live in dignity on their
own soil. In response, the Justice Department,
Bureau of Indian Affairs and corporate land-
grabbers have moved in concert to decapitate
the insurgency. At Wounded Knee, on the eve
of the Ervin hearings on Watergate, 15 armed
personnel carriers with mounted .50 calibre
machine guns surrounded the area. Twenty
tanks were brought in, accompanied by 140
FBI agents and 86 BIA policemen. The 82nd
Airborne was bivouacked nearby. For weeks
the nation watched, expecting—what?
Another Wounded Knee? My Lai? Attica?
Since that time, 135 indictments have been
handed down by federal grand juries; 400
persons have been arrested because they were
on their way to Wounded Knee from other
states, or because they were Indian and federal authorities thought they "might be" on
their way to Wounded Knee.

Attacks on working people are mounting in
intensity. Schoolteachers by the hundreds are
going to jail in defiance of court injunctions.

Hospital organizers are becoming victims of a
campaign of terror. Assassinations and assassination attempts against militant rank-and-
file and union leaders are coming to light
with increasing frequency, the most pub-
licized being the murder of miners' leader
Jock Yablonski. A special campaign has been
aimed at the poorest of the poor workers,
those that harvest the fields. Tactics of that
campaign include: an assassination plot
against farmworkers' leader Cesar Chavez;
massive roundups of Chicanos and Mexican
nationals for deportation to Mexico; Pentagon
purchases in quantity of crops being boycott-
ed; the Nixon-allied Teamsters' collaboration
with growers' associations to destroy the
farmworkers' union; CRP and Teamster donations to American Nazi party members to
organize vigilante actions against union
members; a thousand unionists arrested in
one organizing drive.

The prison system and county jails have
become concentration camps in concrete.
Millions of people languish each day in jails,
stripped of all rights and made to endure
punishment without respite. Long prison
terms are the rule for those without means,
and county and city jails have become preventive detention centers for those who cannot afford bail; this to such an extent that *the
majority of those in jail today have not been
brought to trial.* New techniques of sadism
are being refined in the name of "behavior

modification"; uncooperative inmates are subject to electroshock, drug conditioning, sensory deprivation and psychosurgery. Those who would resist these demeaning conditions are made special victims of torture: At Attica prison in New York, 43 prisoners and prison guards were shot to death in a matter of minutes on orders of governor Nelson Rockefeller. The man who put the massacre into motion will run for reelection while surviving victims have been indicted en masse for murder and related crimes.

Ghettos and barrios are brutalized with mounting intensity as the call from on high goes out for further crackdowns in the name of "law and order." Paramilitary and clandestine branches of local police—like STRESS in Detroit—have become assassination squads, while foot patrolmen in New York and elsewhere are being armed with shotguns, and police and sheriff's departments in virtually every population center are equipped with tanks and armored vehicles. Especially ominous is the organization of "Patrolmen's Benevolent Associations" along the Atlantic seaboard, based on the notion that the judicial process is not nearly so efficient, swift or deadly as a shotgun. Any city of size is sure to retain a police intelligence unit, a Red Squad, organized to infiltrate movements for social justice, to spy, sow division and to entrap. Working in coordination with federal intelligence agencies, the local Red Squads are responsible for the jailings of hundreds and the deaths of dozens of movement activists.[6]

Louis Tackwood, a former Los Angeles police agent, reports that the Ford Foundation, LAPD and the CIA trained men like Ron Karenga to organize jobless young people and demoralized students into assassination teams. Karenga's US organization was responsible for the murders of several Black Panther party leaders. Thus, the "National Caucus of Labor Committees," a group of vigilantes armed to attack liberal and Left groups, includes probation officers, former army intelligence officers and federally-funded youth organizers among its leading cadres. Tackwood has revealed that, as a local police agent, he was in touch with James McCord and E. Howard Hunt to provoke disorders at the Republican Convention when it was originally scheduled for San Diego. His best guess is that the disorders, planned to result in a number of deaths, would have served as the excuse for a Presidential declaration of "national emergen-

[6]John Caulfield and Anthony Ulasewicz, two of the gumshoes who performed dirty tricks as White House secret police, were for years agents of the New York City Red Squad. It may be more than coincidental that Caulfied was known as an "expert in Cuban affairs," especially in light of the early 1973 revelations that the CIA again intervened in U. S. domestic affairs by training the Red Squad in New York in infiltration and surveillance. The New York police are supposed to have some one million dossiers on city residents on file.

cy," and the implementation of the contingency plans for fascism being formulated by McCord's group in the White House basement.[7]

Plausible or not—and who at this time is prepared to reject the possibility on its face—the important point is that the police machinery organized for the purpose of "law and order" and in the name of a New Majority, will ultimately move to eliminate civil law, to impose tyrannical order by a powerful elite over the popular majority. The oppression of minority peoples will surely oppress the majority as well, even if their vision is sufficiently blunted to blind them to this certainty. Similarly, what appears on first glance to repress radical groupings will, with sharper focus, be seen as an attack on the majority. In just this way, what began a couple of generations ago with anti-Communist blacklists has evolved to the point of "enemy lists" in the custody of the White House, on file for retribution—"legal or illegal," in the words of the Presidential chief of staff.

† † †

The thoughtful citizen may by now begin to brood that Watergate is only the tip of the knife. For this is the same government which supported "no-knock" laws, giving police the right to enter homes secretly or by force, in violation of the Fourth Amendment. It has

[7]See McCord, the Roster.

advocated preventive detention—imprisonment without bail of persons on the mere suspicion that they may sometime in the future commit crimes. By such yahoo standards, burglary becomes a "caper," political dossiers collected by the tens of millions are dismissed as an administrative lapse, false arrests by the thousands are disregarded by the Justice Department as an unavoidable inconvenience.

Richard Nixon has stooped to his own level in advocating his new criminal code. In presenting the code's section calling for reinstitution of the death penalty in defiance of his own Supreme Court ("soft-headed judges" were his words), Nixon's attitude might now give him pause for reflection. "Americans in the last decade were often told that the criminal was not responsible for his crimes against society, but that society was responsible," Nixon said. "I totally disagree with this permissive philosophy. Society is guilty of crime only when we fail to bring the criminal to justice. When we fail to make the criminal pay for his crime, we encourage him to think that crime will pay."

Among other provisions of the proposed code is an official secrets act that would delight the Greek junta, providing 10- to 15-year sentences, and fines up to $100,000, for disclosing confidential information; ruled out as a defense is proof that the material—things like "enemies lists"—is improperly classified. This, the President advocated, would be "punishment without pity." The new criminal code would also deny any defense against entrapment by police provocateurs; and reactivate the unconstitutional Smith Act to permit long jail sentences for advocacy of revolutionary doctrine.

One section of the code—the jailing of newspeople for releasing "classified" information—has, even without Congressional approval, been *de facto* implemented by Nixon courts. For the first time in the nation's history, the federal government used prior restraint (in the Pentagon Papers case) as a means of stifling freedom of the press. By abrogating a reporter's right to protect the confidentiality of his sources, the Administration has been responsible for the jailing of the first U. S. newsmen for refusal to surrender rights basic to the conduct of their profession. Another 35 newspeople now face prison for a host of "crimes." Black newsman Earl Caldwell, *The New York Times'* San Francisco reporter, has refused to give the grand jury notes and tapes of confidential interviews conducted while reporting the activities of the Black Panther party; the *Boston Globe's* Washington bureau man, Tom Oliphant, was arrested for covering the flight of a mercy mission airlifting medical supplies to the besieged Wounded Knee; Les Whitten, top assistant to Jack Anderson, was handcuffed and shackled by the FBI undercover agents as he was returning to the Justice Department stolen files from the Bureau of

Indian Affairs, given to him by those who
took them from the BIA; the FBI conducted a
full-scale investigation of CBS's Daniel
Schorr, considered unfriendly by some of Mr.
Nixon's men; Schorr's CBS colleague, Marvin
Kalb, another White House "enemy," had his
office broken into twice in the month of July
1973; *Newsday* reporters had their tax returns
audited because they revealed the shady
business dealings of Nixon companion Bebe
Rebozo; Vice President Agnew has sustained
for five years a determined and vitriolic campaign of denigration of the news media, to
intimidate the press from investigative in-
quiry and to discredit its findings in the eyes
of the public; Nixon claims that "opinion
makers" have a duty to support the President,
while Administration image-makers appeal
to biased local affiliates to reject network
news; the Presidency remains closed to press
penetration in emulation of Nixon mentor
Howard Hughes; the Nixon Supreme Court
ruling on pornography gives each community
its own option on whether to accept the First
Amendment, using as a gauge whether a work
has "serious literary, artistic, political or sci-
entific value," a standard which would allow
the community of, say, San Clemente, to
outlaw the volume you hold in your hands.

[6]

ENEMIES

WHAT Watergate shows, to those who were
unable to catch myriad other signals, is that
U. S. capitalism is in deeper trouble than it
has ever been before. In February 1973 the
dollar was devalued for the second time in 14
months, and within five more months there
was another de facto devaluation of 10 percent in international trading. That one-time
symbol of world economic supremacy—the
Almighty Dollar, Dollar Diplomacy, etc.—has
reached the end of the American Century.
Japan and Western Europe have fully re-
covered from war-time devastation to the
point of serious economic competition with a
United States capitalism overextended
abroad, and with military spending consum-
ing the bulk of the federal budget for a quarter
of a century. For the first time in our history,
war proved disastrous for the economy, a
sure sign of declining strength.

While the United States was tied down in
Indochina, progressive nationalist regimes in
Panama and Peru and a socialist government
in Chile joined Cuba in resisting U. S. hegemony in "our own backyard." Libera-

tion movements gathered increasing support in the Portuguese colonies and white supremist countries in Africa. Palestinian resistance and nationalist movements in the Arab world contended for power with imperialism in the Middle East. The Atlantic capitalist alliance began to unravel, while CENTO and SEATO passed out of practical existence altogether.

These events—combined with the losses in Vietnam in lives, military effect, dollars and balance of payments—caused the dissolution of ruling class unanimity. That new division was brought into the open by popular opposition at home to the war and its domestic effects, particularly on the cities and their ghetto components. The Tet offensive ended the presidency of Lyndon Johnson, and the invasion of Cambodia and domestic outrage at that aggression threatened to make Richard Nixon a one-term President.[1] Detente with the Soviet Union and China served to give people the impression that nuclear peace was indeed at hand, but the new relationships

[1] The Indochina war demonstrated how far the deterioration of democracy had gone. The cold war and the "need" of military adventures abroad placed enormous power into the hands of the executive branch. When majority popular opposition to the war made itself felt, its Congressional expression counted for naught. Notwithstanding the ambivalence of the senators and congressmen, and their basic allegience to the system rather than to their constituencies, it was clear that the President had usurped the power to make war. Con-

also carried with them the danger of increased interest in and contact with the socialist world by U. S. citizens and their organizations. A defensive U. S. capitalism, recognizing that the socialist countries now contain more than 40 percent of world industrial output, may have dictated detente, but its potential political effect on the people had to be blunted.

† † †

We have already shown the growth of state-monopoly capitalism based on military spending during the second world war, its consolidation in the post-war period in the name of anti-Communism, the growth of its police and intelligence apparatus and the

---

gress—the constitutional authority to declare wars—had been circumvented. With the withdrawal of U. S. forces from South Vietnam, the White House moved to eliminate Congressional power to make domestic policy as well. Through the impounding of $40 billion of Congressional allocations, the elimination of legislative social programs and revenue sharing with local areas, the President sought to end the historical checks and balances of the federal system, tipping the balance irretrievably in his direction while he holds all the checks.

Indeed there is good reason to believe it was the continuing U. S. bombardment of Cambodia and the presence of 10,000 U. S. plainclothes "advisors" in South Vietnam, both in violation of the January 1973 peace treaty, that had caused the Watergate case to break wide open. The building constitutional crisis, with a voracious executive usurping congressional and judicial powers unto itself, has been exacerbated by parallel deterioration of democracy.[2] To guarantee the continuity of the *ancien regime*, the CRP began in 1970 to amass a war chest of millions of dollars from the giant corporations[3] through threats of SEC investigations or promises to call off pending hearings, and through government contracts and permits in payment for favors delivered or

---

Nixon's apparent plan to stay in, rather than extricate the U. S. from, Indochina.

[2]The twin development—the growth of corporate power in league with the state apparatus, and the loss of popular prerogatives—is natural. An economic structure based on control of the wealth by a few while the great majority which produces the wealth goes without power, is undemocratic in its essence. Of course, that undemocratic nature will find its reflection in the political structure. Ultimately real democracy will come only with the destruction of such an undemocratic system and the construction of socialism, where those who produce the wealth through their labor also control it. For purposes of this volume, however, we are concerned with the deterioration of democratic liberties—and the movement to defend and expand those liberties—within a fundamentally undemocratic system.

[3]Estimates vary from at least $60 million to far more than $100 million. Chief Nixon fundraisers Maurice Stans and Herbert Kalmbach demanded from several top corporation executives one percent of their net worth. Among the companies approached with this request were American Airlines, Olin Mathieson Chemical, Lockheed Corporation, Ford, Chrysler, Northrup, Litton, Firestone Tire and Rubber, W. R. Grace, IBM, General Electric, General Dynamics, American Express. See Kalmbach and Stans, the Roster.

promised. Nixon had already neutralized
Congress, restructured the Supreme Court
and diminished the influence of even his
cabinet. The White House staff became the
operative arm of government. Watergate
shows that he had also brought the intelligence agencies, foreign and domestic, under
his aegis by placing personal friends and
political cronies in their leadership. Now
with a new unlimited fund of CRP dollars,
and cooperation of the highest agencies of
government, the White House put together a
private police force, protected by the FBI and
Justice Department. This secret para-military
operation would use blackmail, tax audits,[4]
burglary, mail and telephone interference,
assault and battery, kidnapping and related
crimes. First targets were to be the antiwar
movement, and the liberation movements of
Blacks and other oppressed minorities, and
new movements of labor militancy. And,
coupled with overt White House attacks on
the loyal opposition—the liberal Congressional bloc and the press—the secret police
would act clandestinely against the opposition. They would create a "new majority" by
eliminating or neutralizing all opponents.[5]

[4] In 1972 alone, at least 915 illegal tax audits were
conducted against White House "enemies."
[5] After earlier wars, the country was driven by repression to the Right to consolidate imperialist gains and to
win unanimous public support. After the first world
war, the terror campaign against the Left opposition

If the U. S. government could do this abroad for three-quarters of a century, why not at home, and for the same reasons: economic plunder free of organized opposition.[6] The spectre of fascism—supported by the United States in Portugal and Paraguay, South Korea and South Africa, Iran and Indonesia—would begin to come home to haunt us. For what is fascism if not monopoly capitalism void of democratic avenues of expression? This particular President had always had closet flirtations with fascist groupings and he had never had a particular bent for brooking opposition views. Besides, democracy was popular, and as Richard Nixon reminds us in each fireside chat, he does not do "the popular thing."

But Nixon is also a creature of his chosen system, and capitalism does not opt for fas-

---

was symbolized by the Palmer raids, mass roundups and deportations; after the second world war, McCarthyism and the Cold War were used. But imperialism had lost and continued to lose in Indochina. To sustain popular support or acquiescence now meant turning the defeat into a victory, into "peace with honor." With the manipulated POWs and little else on his side, Nixon had to still those who would take exception to his propaganda.

[6]Those who argue that for the Watergaters money was not a factor should know that corporate profits in the U. S. *after taxes* amounted to an annual rate of $57 billion in the last quarter of 1972 and in the first and second quarters of 1973 to $70 billion. In Chapter 5 we listed some of the incredible increases in profits for January-March 1973, the first quarter after Nixon's reelection.

cism except as a last resort, to retain power in the face of revolutionary crisis. (That the Nixon White House chose to go in the direction of fascism may in part be a paranoid misreading on its part of the antiwar and democratic opposition as a revolutionary opposition.) Capitalism, if it had its choices, would prefer to govern with the consent of the governed. And how capitalism should govern in these times is precisely what is at issue in the political polarization of the ruling class today.[7]

Obviously we do not have fascism, or there would be no Watergate exposure, nor essays like this one printed (and read) openly. But just as obviously, there are powerful forces at work that would move us in that direction. Unlike Germany in the early 1930s, the main fascist elements of our society are not on the

[7]As we have seen, the ascendancy to world capitalist hegemony after World War Two was accompanied by political solidarity within the ranks of big capitalism at home. The differences that have expressed themselves so openly around Watergate are easy enough to discern although the breakdown of economic forces is unclear. (As one commentator has noted, "Ruling classes are not in the habit of calling meetings and publishing minutes.") Some hold that the split is between the so-called New Money of the West and the South (as represented by Richard Nixon) and the Eastern Establishment. But that doesn't explain the presence of Dr. Kissinger, the main foreign policy analyst for the Rockefeller interests, directing U. S. foreign policy. In fact, the Nixon reelection campaign brought the monopolies together for the moment, faced with the uncertain choice represented by McGovern.

fringes of the political spectrum but have
emerged from the heart of it. George Dimi-
trov, the Bulgarian Communist who formulated the concept of the anti-fascist united
front, warned that, "Before the establishment
of a fascist dictatorship, bourgeois[8] governments usually pass through a number of
preliminary stages and adopt a number of
reactionary measures which directly facili-
tate the accession to power of fascism." Dimi-
trov continued, "Whoever does not fight the
reactionary measures of the bourgeoisie and
the growth of fascism at these preparatory
stages is not in a position to prevent the
victory of fascism, but on the contrary, facili-
tates that victory."

The "reactionary measures" at this particular "preparatory stage" that need most to be
fought, all appeal to anti-Communism and
racism as their most potent ideological weap-
on. It is more than coincidence that the
"Watergate 110"[9] are all white men. One
would think, from the contemporary socio-
logical literature which "proves" an inherent
criminality of racial minorities, that at least
one Black or Chicano or Puerto Rican or
Native American or Asian-American would
be found within the biggest criminal conspiracy. But scratch as one will, not a single

[8]Dimitrov, of course, used the Marxist definition of
bourgeosie as the class that owns the means of production, and not the common modern U. S. usage to denote
an amorphous middle class.
[9]See the Roster.

person of color is to be found. Rather, the conspirators were, to a man, racists seeking to fix the blame of the system's crisis on its worst victims, thereby excusing from responsibility its true perpetrators.

We have seen how the many and varied legal and illegal methods of repression, now used against the general public, were first developed and refined for use against the most conscious components of the people, against the Left and the radicalized elements of the working class, in the first place the oppressed minorities. We have seen that those who are responsible for the Watergate conspiracy have concentrated Black and Brown people into urban ghettos, virtual armed camps with tanks, artillery and modern military weaponry in the hands of the police forces. White people, who do not understand that those same guns will turn on them, avoid resistance to racism at their own peril.

Perhaps the greatest victim of the centuries of racism—victimized more than ever during the decade of the Vietnam war—is the public consciousness. White sensibilities are so brutalized as to be twisted at times beyond human recognition. The Watergate revelations would have unquestionably brought down any parliamentary government in Europe. But after the horror of Vietnam with its equivalent of two Hiroshima bombs a week, each week for years, its sadistic torture of hundreds of thousands, its napalming and terror bombings of civilian populations, all being shown nightly on television accompanied by body-count scoreboards—after all this, we are prepared to accept virtually any crime that isn't aimed directly at us, and many that are. Violence and corruption have become an accepted way of life for most of our people. This acquiescence, coupled with racism, presents a frightening setting for the possibility of fascism.

† † †

But Vietnam taught us more, not least of which is the role of liberalism as an ideological buffer to fundamental change. A CBS television reporter, covering the 1973 New York city mayoral primary elections, commented: "The shadow of Watergate hovers over all. People now distrust the system, and this is a tragedy. For this is the only system we've got. We have to make it work." Far from a tragedy, the massive distrust of the system is one of the more encouraging aspects of Watergate. It would indeed be a "tragedy" to try to make work a system long inoperative. The crisis of the economic system of capitalism is also a crisis of its political prop, the two-party system. The Cold War, the Korean war, the invasion of Cuba, Vietnam, institutionalized racism, Phases One, Two, Three and Four, the buildup of giant intelligence agencies to record our every movement, the police departments to repress movements for social change—all have been bi-partisan efforts, as they like to

say. Even with the crimes of Watergate revealed, the more "enlightened" liberal poli-
ticians like former Defense Secretary Clark
Clifford and Wisconsin Democratic Congressman Henry Reuss, have proposed as a way
out of the crisis the formation of a "government of national unity," a fusion administration of Democrats and Republicans. The one
virtue in the proposal is that it would make
the two-party system into a one-party system,
and appearances would no longer deceive.
But it won't wash. For Watergate is the cul-
mination of a bipartisan effort, three decades
long.

What Watergate signifies is that the class
that rules our country through the Republican and Democratic parties is unable to meet
the needs and demands of the people for
quality education and medical care as a
human right, for an end to wars and the
elimination of the enormous tax burden carried by those who can least afford it. Unable
to meet popular needs, they resort to illegal
police methods to still popular demands.
Today in Washington an honest man is de-
fined as one who confesses his crimes. This is
the class that "almost stole America," in the
words of Senator Lowell Weicker.

The attempt to steal the country is ongoing
and can only be thwarted by an organized
democratic opposition, independent of the
two capitalist parties. There are undoubtedly
men and women of decency and integrity in
both parties, but the two parties are indelibly

marked with the corruption that resulted in
Watergate. It takes no great insight to know
that the Eugene McCarthy and George
McGovern campaigns, headed by candidates
who had no quarrel with the basic system of
capitalism, were sabotaged from the outset by
the leaders and financial backers of their
party. Only movements independent of the
two parties, varied in form, can fundamentally change the situation. One of those
forms would have to be a political party—
based in the first place among working people
of all colors—that would organize to contend
for power.

Those that argue that mass sentiment has
no effect upon decisions from on high should
be disabused, in light of weekly bulletins
from the White House denying that the President will resign. The millions of citizens
who marched in the streets against the Vietnam war and went home disillusioned because "demonstrations have no effect,"
should learn, if nothing else from the Watergate investigations, that their demonstrations
drove one President out of office and almost
drove his successor bananas.

That mass sentiment and those demonstrations, organized into an independent political party, could play an historical role in the
wake of Watergate. Congress will not im-
peach the Nixon administration nor call for
new elections without massive popular intervention. (As landlords of the White House,
the people also retain the right to evict ten-

ants who breech their contract.) Neither will
the two major parties end the domestic cold
war, nor abolish the repressive and anti-
Communist legislation which gave impetus
to Watergate. A thorough investigation of the
activities of the CIA, FBI and the Pentagon
can only be made by a people's tribunal; the
Congress we have will not bite the hand
which feeds it. Opening up the records of
those agencies would result in their abolition,
and nothing could be more in our *real* national security interests; but those books will
remain closed, and those departments operating, in the absence of an organized movement
from below. Out of the Watergate investigations Congress will undoubtedly pass some
new election reform legislation, but only con-
certed massive public demand can bring
about real electoral change: outlawing private
donations to election campaigns; giving a set
amount of government money (perhaps one
million dollars) to *every* political party on the
ballot; abolishing anti-Communist and other
laws which prohibit smaller parties from
ballot status; giving equal television and
radio time for *each* candidate on the ballot.

† † †

One of the more appalling pieces of political lunacy to be revealed by the Watergate
investigations was the existence of a White
House "enemies list" of real or imagined
tormentors of Richard Nixon. Prepared in the
office of Nixon special counsel Charles Colson, the list of enemies—to be subjected to

tax audits for potential blackmail and other harassments—included 31 Democratic "politicoes," among them the entire Congressional Black Caucus; 18 organizations ranging from the National Welfare Rights Organization to Common Cause; 14 labor officials; 21 scholars; 52 businessmen and political fund contributors; a dozen celebrities; and 56 television reporters and political writers. Among the last named was *The New York Times'* columnist Tom Wicker. Wicker commented in response: "Once indignation and the fear has passed, the temptation to laugh had been overcome, and puzzlement had turned to sadness, I knew I belonged on those lists. Of such people as those who compiled them, and the man they served so zealously, who would not be an enemy?"

THE   ROSTER:

The Watergate 110[1]

THE WATERGATE "affair," as the more cautious
of the press corps have dubbed recent events,
has brought the careers of certain public and
no-so-public personalities under scrutiny.
What follows is an alphabetical listing of
those with very direct connections to the
matter.

[1]A popular lapel pin now reads, "Free the Watergate
500." In fact, as this book seeks to demonstrate, the
Watergate "500" is the "executive committee" of those
who run this country—the giant corporations who
control our wealth and their political spokesmen. The
listings in this Roster include only those who have
come to public light since the Watergate arrests. We can
see the convergence in the backgrounds of the personalities sketched here of ties to big corporations and
government offices (Securities and Exchange Commission, Departments of Justice, State, Agriculture, Treasury, Commerce, Defense, the White House and National Security Council) with police and intelligence
agencies (local Red Squads, CIA, FBI, AEC, NSA).
   All of the facts in this roster, unless otherwise noted,
have been reported in the Chicago *Sun-Times*, Los
Angeles *Times, Newsweek,* New York *Post, The New
York Times, Time,* and the Washington *Post.* The
information on organized crime and Bebe Rebozo
comes primarily from *SunDance* (Nov.–Dec. 1972),

Robert H. Abplanalp. Creator and owner of the aerosol spray valve, Abplanalp has a personal net worth of over $100 million. His company, Precision Valve, Inc., was recommended by Justice Department staffers for investigation of pricing practices in 1971, but the investigation was vetoed from the top of the Department. His business was handled by Richard Nixon's New York law firm, but his relationship with Nixon runs far deeper than that of a business associate. One of the two islands he owns in the Bahamas, Grand Cay, serves as a Nixon retreat, the President occupying the master suite in Abplanalp's home. He also owns a plot of land, together with Charles "Bebe" Rebozo,† adjoining Nixon's Florida "White House" in Key Biscayne. (Another close neighbor is ITT chairman Harold Geneen.) Abplanalp bought the Key Biscayne property from an Indianapolis couple who said they were being harassed by the Secret Service. He paid $150,000 for the estate. By 1977 Abplanalp will have received all of his purchase price back in government rentals, and the government will have protected and improved the property with well over a million dollars of repairs and furnishings, while the value of the land has risen spectacularly. Although the family assistance

NACLA Newsletter (Oct. 1972), and *New York Review of Books* (May 3, 1973).

Throught this roster, the sign † signifies that the person noted is also to be found in this alphabetical listing.

plan, calling for a guaranteed $2400 annual
income for a family of four, was dropped by
Nixon because it challenged the work ethic,
this did not deter Abplanalp's plan for assist-
ing the President's family of four. The "Western White House," Nixon's home in San
Clemente, California, was bought by Abplanalp's $625,000 "loan" to Nixon, a loan
that needn't be paid back. In addition, Abplanalp paid another $1.25 million for the
land adjacent to Nixon's, which he has
thoughtfully turned over to the latter. U. S.
taxpayers paid about $460,000 more to fix up
the estate, under a renovation program with
the code name "Operation Sunrise." The
President even paid $33,500 of his own for
the $2 million house. (See Richard Nixon.†)
The deal was handled by Herbert Kalmbach†
in his capacity as Nixon's personal lawyer.
Abplanalp is also a financial patron of New
York Conservative Party Senator James Buck-
ley.

Spiro Agnew. Vice-President of the United
States, 1969–197-. He announced on April
25, 1973, when it became clear that John
Dean,† H. R. Haldeman,† John Ehrlichman,†
and Richard Kleindienst† were leaving the
White House inner sanctum, that he had "full
confidence in the integrity of President Nixon." He is now under investigation by the
U. S. Attorney and by IRS on charges of bribery, extortion and tax fraud during the period
he was Baltimore county executive (1962-7),

Governor of Maryland (1967–8) and Vice
President. Kickbacks while he was governor
were reported to be about $1000 a week, and
he is accused of taking another $50,000 while
Vice President. Also under investigation is a
member of his staff, Jerome Wolff, who was
president of Greiner Environmental Services
(under investigation in Florida as well as
Maryland) and named by Governor Agnew to
be chairman of the state roads commission.
Still another subject of the investigation is J.
Walter Jones, an Annapolis banker and chief
fundraiser for the Maryland CRP in 1972.
Agnew's office housed Dean during the latter's efforts to cover up the ITT scandal (See
Dean below.) He was himself implicated in
secret ITT papers regarding an anti-trust fix
when he intervened in favor of ITT to obtain
Securities and Exchange Commission approval of the takeover of Hartford Fire Insurance Co., in violation of the Sherman
Anti-Trust Act. Agnew also attended a party
in 1970 at the home of Interior Secretary
Rogers C. B. Morton (at the time Republican
national chairman), together with John
Mitchell,† ITT chairman Harold Geneen and
others, to discuss the ITT deal. After the
National Guard shot down four student on-
lookers at a Kent State (Ohio) University
demonstration against the U. S. invasion of
Cambodia, he called the students "bums." A
"Salute to Ted Agnew" testimonial during
the 1972 presidential campaign was beefed

up with $50,000 unreported CRP funds, to
hide the failure of expected receipts at the
fund-raising dinner. (See William Mills.)
Agnew has led the White House attack on the
Senate investigation of Watergate, along lines
similar to his earlier campaign against the
press which, despite that campaign, opened
up the case for public scrutiny.

Gerald Alch. Law partner of F. Lee Bailey†
and originally the attorney for James
McCord.† Said by McCord to have asked that
he blame the Central Intelligence Agency
(CIA) for the Watergate break-in in return for
clemency from the President.

Robert H. Allen. The chairman of Gulf Resources and Chemical Corporation in Texas
and chairman of the Texas branch of the
Finance Committee to Re-elect the President
(FCRP). He gave $100,000 in unreported
anonymous donations to CRP, part of which
helped pay for the Watergate burglary and
cover-up. The money was routed through
Mexico for "laundering," a process used to
change money so as to hide original sources,
with help from Kenneth Dahlberg,† the
White Tornado of GOP politics. The money
eventually found its way into Bernard Bark-
ers† Miami bank account, another modern
washday miracle. John Connolly† is the
attorney for Allen's Gulf Resources and
Chemical Corporation. Following Allen's
contributions to CRP, the government's En-

vironmental Protection Agency backed off on a threat to impose stiffer pollution controls on a major Gulf Resources subsidiary.

Dwayne Andreas. Popularly known as the "Soybean King," he is president of Archer-Daniels-Midland Co., the largest domestic soybean processer, in which capacity he is defendant in a pending antitrust suit for illegally acquiring two other soybean companies. A close friend and financial supporter of Hubert Humphrey, in 1972 he hedged his political bets by also supporting Richard Nixon. It was his $25,000, given to Dahlberg, which wound up in Barker's bank account as payoff for the Watergate burglary. He also serves as a director, with Dahlberg, of the National City Bank in Minneapolis. His Seaview Hotel in Bal Harbour, Florida, kept the Dahlberg check for Barker. He also serves as a member of the board of Radio Free Europe. As a result of his $120,000 total donations to CRP, he received a new Minneapolis bank charter in record time and in avoidance of Minnesota state scrutiny.

Roy L. Ash. Originally recruited to the White House by H. R. Haldeman,† he now serves as director of the Office of Management and Budget, presiding over $268 billion of our money. Ash used to be comptroller for Hughes Aircraft (see Howard Hughes), for whom he got the U. S. Air Force to pay an extra $43 million above that called for in a contract, through questionable accounting methods. He left Hughes to found Litton Industries, of which he became president. Here he received a $130 million loan from the state of Mississippi to finance "a shipyard of the future"; with cost overruns, the U. S. Navy poured another $3 billion into the shipyard. Another Ash deal was as interesting: he swapped 22 acres of California seacoast land for 14,145 acres of Nevada ranch land in 1969, the only such arrangement allowed by Nixon's Department of Interior. With the deal, Ash tripled his money in five years. He is now under SEC investigation for violating regulations against trading stock on the basis of "insiders" information by unloading 86,000 shares of common stock in a failing company.

F. Lee Bailey. Law partner of Alch.† Bailey won acquittal for Captain Ernest Medina, who led the massacre of the My Lai hamlet in South Vietnam, and was James Earl Ray's attorney in the Martin Luther King assassination case, in which he urged Ray to plead guilty against Ray's will. Ray was sentenced to life without possibility of parole. Bailey is now under indictment with Glen W. Turner† on 28 counts of mail fraud and conspiracy.

Alfred C. Baldwin III. A former FBI agent, he served as bodyguard to Martha Mitchell, wife of John Mitchell.† During the 1972 election campaign he worked for the CRP under James McCord,† for whom he spied on Senators Edmund Muskie, Edward Kennedy, Mike

Gravel, William Proxmire, Charles Percy and Jacob Javits; and on members of the House Edward Koch, Shirley Chisholm and Pete McCloskey. He also infiltrated the Vietnam Veterans Against the War (VVAW) for McCord, in order to provoke violence at the Republican national convention in Miami in August 1972, thus giving justification for the Watergate break-in two months earlier. This would have been perhaps the first case on record of "preventive strike" *after* the fact. Baldwin was a member of the Watergate bugging team, in which capacity he transcribed the tapes. He was given immunity from prosecution in return for becoming a government witness.

Bernard L. Barker. His long road to Watergate began in Cuba where, as a member of dictator Fulgencio Batista's secret police, he served as liaison with the FBI and U. S. Treasury Department. When the Cuban Revolution came to power he fled to Miami, where he joined the CIA and served as quartermaster, under the code name "Macho", for the mercenary invasion of Cuba at the Bay of Pigs. He recruited the other Cuban exiles used in the Watergate break-in and was convicted for his role. But before Watergate he was part of the White House team under E. Howard Hunt† and G. Gordon Liddy†, which formed the core of Nixon's private intelligence army. Among his accomplishments were participation in the burglary of Dr. Lewis Fielding, psychiatrist of Pentagon

Papers defendant Daniel Ellsberg; leading a seven-man team of *gusanos* to physically attack Ellsberg when the latter spoke to a Washington D. C. antiwar rally, while J. Edgar Hoover's body was lying in state nearby; and burglarizing (according to John Dean†), the Chilean Embassy in Washington. For his efforts he received from CRP $114,000 in his Miami bank account, and another $47,000 in cash from Hunt's wife, Dorothy. Before his CRP involvement, Barker was a real estate partner with Bebe Rebozo† and a part-time business partner with Hunt, with investments in Chile, Dominican Republic, Nicaragua, and Panama.

Robert E. Bennett. Son of Wallace Bennett, conservative Republican Senator from Utah. He used to share a desk with Hunt at Robert Mullen† and Co., where he did public relations work for Howard Hughes.† Bennett gave Hunt a blank check for CRP from Hughes. He also used to share a desk at Mullen with Douglas Caddy,† the original Watergate attorney and co-funder of Young Americans for Freedom.

Robert Benz. President of the Tampa (Fla.) Young Republicans, he was hired by Donald Segretti† to plan disruptions of the Henry Jackson and Edmund Muskie campaigns in Florida.

Peter Brennan. Richard Nixon's second-term Secretary of Labor. As the head of the New

York construction workers, he had been the most outspoken labor leader against integrated hiring practices in the building trades. He organized the "hard-hat" demonstration of right-wing construction workers to beat up N. Y. antiwar demonstrators in return for Nixon's promise not to enforce anti-discrimination laws in federally-funded building programs. At the urging of Charles Colson,† Nixon invited Brennan to the White House to present the President with a "hard hat." Even as Labor Secretary, he carries on his person a pearl-handled revolver, for which he has been given U. S. Marshal's credentials. The organizer for CRP of a committee of 200 labor officials for Nixon, he has called Watergate "just politics."

Earl Butz. Secretary of Agriculture and the primary Nixon spokesman against consumer movements protesting runaway food prices. Butz has said: "In this current flap about food prices, there is a growing feeling among many Americans and organizations that cheap food is their birthright. The opportunity to earn profits is what the farming business is all about." He spoke to the Lehigh Valley Cooperative Farmers, the Pennsylvania dairy interests, on the day they made a secret $50,000 cash donation to the CRP through Jeb Stuart Magruder.† Butz was also a leading official of Ralston-Purina, one of the nation's largest food processors.

J. Fred Buzhardt. Now White House special

counsel overseeing Watergate-related matters, he has been pressuring special prosecutor Archibald Cox to combat publicity adverse to Nixon. During John Dean's† testimony before the Ervin Senate committee investigating Watergate, Buzhardt sent to panel member Senator Daniel Inouye a White House brief answering Dean's charges and a number of questions for crossexamination, so that "the White House can have its day in court." The brief and questions were later disavowed by the White House. A few days later Buzhardt claimed that Nixon, "like all of us," is confused by Watergate and doesn't know what to think or whom to believe. Previously chief counsel for the Department of Defense, he testified untruthfully during the prosecution of the Pentagon Papers case. While serving as Pentagon trouble-shooter, he refused to let the generals appear before Ervin's constitutional rights subcommittee, which was investigating the Army's domestic intelligence activities, including its following and keeping files on millions of civilians. Earlier he had served eight years as administrative aide to South Carolina Senator Strom Thurmond. Buzhardt's father is Thurmond's law partner.

Douglas Caddy. A co-founder of Young Americans for Freedom, he was a close friend and co-worker of Hunt at Mullen and Co. On pre-arranged instructions from Hunt, Caddy was the original Watergate defendants' lawyer, but was found in contempt of court for refusing to answer grand jury questions.

William J. Casey. Was chairman of the SEC at the time G. Bradford Cook† deleted mention of the $200,000 cash gift from Robert Vesco† to CRP. Casey met four times with Vesco, on the urging of John Mitchell. While SEC head, he ignored a staff recommendation that the Commission file charges of fraud against ITT during the takeover of Hartford Fire Insurance. He is now under investigation for perjury and falsification of records for defying the House Commerce Committee which oversees SEC; when the House committee demanded documents relating to ITT's $400,000 gift to CRP in return for SEC dropping the antitrust case against ITT, Casey turned the documents over to the Justice Department instead. The Justice Department, of course, was being run by CRP chief John Mitchell. Casey is now one of 17 defendants in a $2.1 million federal damage suit for self-dealings for personal gain at the expense of a corporation which went bankrupt a week after Casey was nominated to be SEC chairman. Casey presently is Undersecretary of State.

John J. Caulfield. For 10 years a member of the New York police intelligence Red Squad, Caulfield came to Nixon's attention when he served as bodyguard for the candidate's visit to New York during the 1968 campaign. The next year he was working on the White House staff, ostensibly helping to supervise the Intelligence Evaluation Committee under John Dean. Most of his time, however, was spent under John Ehrlichman's† direction, performing "dirty tricks": placing an illegal wiretap on the phone of syndicated columnist Joseph Kraft; breaking into the Brookings Institution; questioning My Lai veterans to find a basis for challenging news reports of the atrocity; with the help of Anthony Ulasewicz† investigating House Speaker Carl Albert's drinking habits, the background of Ted Kennedy's Chappaquiddick accident, the homosexual brother of another Democratic candidate and other such matters. Caulfield was a bodyguard for John Mitchell during the 1972 campaign and worked for CRP using the cover of "advisor on the Administration's law enforcement program." He was the White House intermediary to McCord in offering the latter clemency from the President in return for shifting the blame for Watergate onto the CIA. Until May 1973, Caulfield was assistant director for criminal enforcement of the Treasury Department's Alcohol, Tobacco and Firearms Bureau.

Dwight L. Chapin. An advertising protege of Haldeman, he worked under the latter in 1962 during Nixon's campaign for governor of California. Until February 1973 he worked directly under Haldeman as Nixon's deputy assistant and appointments secretary. He brought Gordon Strachan,† a classmate at the University of Southern California, into the

White House. And he recruited Donald Segretti,† another USC friend, for CRP. Segretti's espionage and sabotage efforts were made under Chapin's instructions. Chapin is now director of market planning for United Air Lines.

Leo Cherne. Director of Freedom House, a right-wing "social democrat" anti-communist organization. Cherne is another Key Biscayne neighbor of Nixon, and was vice-chairman of the "Democrats for Nixon" under John Connolly.† He sent out 10,000 copies of a letter for CRP attacking McGovern's foreign policy; the letter used State Department mailing labels, in violation of federal election rules.

Murray Chotiner. A close campaign advisor to Nixon throughout his long political career, Chotiner also has been an attorney in 267 separate cases for organized crime interests in Southern California. He served as White House counsel until 1971, and admits interceding with Haldeman for Teamster leader Jimmy Hoffa's parole. Chotiner was reported to be, together with Hunt and Liddy, involved in collecting $1.1 million in donations from the Teamsters and Las Vegas gambling interests, a charge Chotiner denies. His Washington law firm, Reeves and Harrison, is located one floor above the CRP offices, which are themselves down the hall from the D. C. office of Mudge, Rose, Guthrie and

Alexander, the Wall Street firm for which Nixon, Mitchell,† Garment,† and Strachan all worked at one point in time. Reeves and Harrison represents several large dairy trusts, and Chotiner arranged for the huge contributions to CRP from the dairy combines in return for fixing higher milk prices.

Ken W. Clawson. Although his White House position was deputy director of communications under Herbert Klein† (now under Ronald Ziegler†), during the 1972 presidential campaign he reported to Colson. He admits forging a letter to a New Hampshire newspaper, during the state's primary, attributing to Edmund Muskie the use of the word "Canuck", a derogatory term for French Canadians, who make up that state's largest minority. He also helped locate the alcoholic brother of another Democratic presidential candidate, to be used for news stories.

William Colby. The new CIA director. He served three years in Vietnam where he organized Operation Phoenix, a clandestine program of mass murder, in which 55,000 Vietnamese men, women and children were killed by CIA assassination teams. He then became overall CIA director for Asia, during which time he oversaw the secret wars in Laos and Thailand and the illicit drug traffic through Southeast and Central Asia, including the use of Air America, the CIA airline, for drug transportation. Until his recent appointment he was deputy director of operations for CIA, in charge of the so-called department of dirty tricks.

William B. Colsey III. The chairman of the Executive Club, a secret Republican party fund-raising organization in New Jersey. The club collected $1000 from at least 149 business and industrial executives, money which was never reported to the Government Accounting Office. He set up non-existent fronts, e.g. the "Political Surveys and Analysis, Inc." and "New Jersey Republican Convention Fund," with false addresses and no records kept. Colsey has been indicted on charges of bribery involving the use of state funds in connection with another, local, political campaign.

Charles W. Colson. The youngest Marine company commander ever, Colson displays on his wall a Green Beret poster which declares, "If you've got 'em by the ---, their hearts and minds will follow." He claims three personal heroes: Lieut. Gen. Lewis Puller ("the greatest blood and guts marine who ever walked"), John Wayne and Richard M. Nixon. Not enough can be said about Colson, but perhaps what follows will suffice. Among his many and varied activities as special counsel to the President, Colson: 1) hired for White House duties his friend and fellow Brown University alumnus E. Howard Hunt, who coordinated the Watergate burglary; 2) paid Hunt and Liddy for the burglary of

Ellsberg psychiatrist Dr. Lewis Fielding;
asked Hunt to break into Arthur Bremer's
Milwaukee apartment after the latter shot
Governor George Wallace (the pretext for the
proposed burglary was to find evidence of
links between Bremer and radical groups, but
considering other Nixon attempts to remove
Wallace from the 1972 election race there are
some who speculate that the idea of the
break-in was to remove incriminating evidence of a conspiracy); 3) organized paid
public rallies in support of Nixon's mining of
Haiphong harbor; 4) paid for forged telegram-
med greetings of support of the mining, to
distort public opinion counts; 5) wrote a
phony advertisement in *The New York Times*
criticizing the *Times'* opposition to the mining; 6) ordered Hunt to forge State Department cables to demonstrate John F. Kennedy's complicity in the assassination of
South Vietnamese dictator Diem; 7) was instrumental in formulating Nixon strategy toward organized labor, including at one point
sending 40 operatives to the 1971 AFL-CIO
convention to contrive a confrontation between that body and Nixon; and at another,
arranging for Brennan† to come to the White
House to give Nixon a hard hat; and at still
another, serving as intermediary between
Nixon and Teamster president Frank Fitzsim-
mons† (Colson is now the lawyer for the
Teamsters); on behalf of Brennan, when the
latter was head of the New York Building
Trades Council, he attempted to prevent

Clayton Cotrell, a Black opponent of the
"New York Plan" for token minority hiring in
construction, from becoming the Labor Department's regional director for New York
(When Brennan became Labor Secretary, Cotrell was removed from his position); he also
made promises on behalf of Nixon that there
would not be any enforcement of anti-
discrimination laws if the construction
unions would support the re-election campaign; 8) was an early and ardent advocate
of the Watergate operation, according to
Magruder; 9) recruited young men to pose as
homosexual supporters of McGovern to link
the latter up with gay liberationists; 10)
ordered the investigation into Ted Kennedy's
private life and the circumstances surround-
ing Chappaquiddick; and arranged for the CRP
to supply disguises and equipment for the
task; 11) organized at least 30 groups of Nixon
supporters to attack network news correspondents through write-in, telephone and
telegram campaigns to local affiliates; 12)
organized the artifical "Vietnam Veterans for
a Just Peace" to try to neutralize public support for the legitimate Vietnam Veterans
Against the War; 13) engineered the destruction of VVAW spokesman John Kerry's congressional campaign in Colson's home Massachusetts district, by quashing an SEC investigation of Kerry's main opponent (Colson's
father is SEC attorney in Boston); 14) was
responsible for naming G. Bradford Cook† as
SEC chairman; 15) planted story in *Life* mag-

azine falsely accusing Maryland's liberal Senator Joseph Tydings of illegal stock manipulation, causing Tydings' defeat at the polls; 16) paid Liddy his $100 a day consultant fees; 17) urged the burglary and firebombing of the Brookings office of Morton Halperin, an Ellsberg friend and former aide to Henry Kissinger;† 18) according to Dean† aide Roy Kinsey, demanded of IRS a list of all contributors to the National Council of Senior Citizens, which works for higher social security benefits and national health insurance; and contributors to Vietnam Veterans Against the War, and Common Cause; 19) directed secret service agents assigned to Muskie and McGovern during the 1972 election campaign to report the candidates' activities to the White House. Colson was the keeper of the White House "enemies list" to be "screwed by the federal machinery." At one time Nixon's liason with congress and special interest groups for pet Nixon projects like the antiballastic missile and the supersonic transport plane, he is now the lawyer for Grumman Aerospace. Colson has bosted to the press, "I would walk over my grandmother if it were necessary" to re-elect Richard Nixon.

John B. Connolly, The former Governor of Texas served as Nixon's first-term Secretary of Treasury, but left the government to become national chairman of the ersatz "Democrats for Nixon." Since the Watergate revelations, he performed an act of "charity" by becoming a Republican and coming to the White House as Nixon's Special Assistant, which one commentator likened to "signing on as cabin boy aboard the Titanic." After one month on the job, he quit. Connolly's instincts, however, are hardly charitable. As a lawyer, he represents the Gulf Resources and Chemical Corporation, now under investigation by a federal grand jury for illegal contributions to CRP of $100,000 routed through Mexico for "laundering" on the way to Maurice Stans'† cash cache. Connolly is also implicated in the ITT antitrust fix by his intervention for government approval of the takeover of Hartford Fire Insurance (see Casey, above). After leaving the Treasury Department, Connolly's law firm got Occidental Petroleum's business, the latter having received Nixon's approval for a massive natural gas deal with the Soviet Union. Simultaneously, Connolly is a director of the Halliburton Company, parent company of Brown and Root, Inc., the worldwide construction firm representing Occidental Petroleum and El Paso Natural Gas. Brown and Root, Inc. is now under grand jury investigation for illegal campaign contributions to a secret Texas CRP fund totalling $700,000 in cash.

G. Bradford Cook. At the time of the Vesco investigation, he was director of SEC market relations, and at the time of the ITT investigation he turned ITT documents over to the

White House instead of the House Commerce Committee, an act contemptuous of Congress. What better qualifications for chairman of the SEC, which Nixon named him on the suggestion of Colson. His tenure, however, lasted only 74 days before he resigned after being accused of deleting references in the SEC investigation to Vesco's $200,000 gift to CRP. Before leaving the SEC, he hired as the Commission's general counsel Lawrence Nerheim, who had been recommended by Rev. Billy Graham, Nixon advisor on spiritual matters and whose multimillion-dollar religious empire Nerheim represents.

General Robert Cushman, Jr. Commandant of the U. S. Marine Corps and a member of the Joint Chiefs of Staff. During Nixon's second term as Vice-President, he was the Veep's chief advisor on national security. It was during this period that Nixon was instrumental in setting into motion the 1961 Bay of Pigs invasion. Through working together at the time, Cushman became associated with Hunt, the CIA's man in the operation, and for nearly 15 years they have had a working relationship. A close friend of Nixon, he was sent to Vietnam to preside over 167,000 troops, the largest number ever commanded by a Marine officer. Cushman became Deputy Director of the CIA during Nixon's first term, and it was he that authorized the CIA false identification papers and disguises, at the request of Ehrlichman, that were used by Hunt and Liddy in their bag job of Ellsberg's doctor, Lewis Fielding.

Kenneth Dahlberg. A multimillionaire industrialist, he served as chairman of the Minnesota CRP and was then the Republican party's chief midwest fund-raiser. A director of the Minneapolis National City Bank, owned by Dwayne Andreas,† Dahlberg was the one who got the $25,000 check from Andreas which turned up in Barker's bank account.

Allen Dorfman. A man with a string of Mafia ties, Dorfman turned over to Mitchell hundreds of thousands of dollars as a donation to CRP from the Teamsters' union. He also arranged for the meeting between Mafia bosses and Teamsters' president Frank Fitzsimmons. Dorfman is now in prison for jury tampering and pension fund frauds.

John W. Dean III. In his early 30s, which is young by most measures for a chief counsel to the President, Dean brought to the White House the necessary credentials for his job: he had held one job in private practice for less than a year, having been dismissed for unethical behavior. When he came to the government in 1969, he became John Mitchell's trouble-shooter in the Justice Department, where he served as deputy under Richard Kleindienst's† authority, responsible for liaison with the Congress. He was appointed chief presidential counsel in April 1970 and lasted there exactly two years. During this time he became White House expert on the doctrine of executive privilege, under which Nixon declined to give information or let aides give information on vital public affairs to Congress or the public. He also has, among others, the following credits: 1) Working out of Agnew's office, he directed the cover-up of the ITT bribery; gave ITT the memo from its lobbyist Dita Beard, spelling out details of the deal, which he had gotten from L. Patrick Gray†; ordered Robert S. Mardian† to investigate columnist Jack Anderson, who broke the story; suppressed the 34 cartons of documents ITT had supplied under subpoena to the SEC, including memos showing Mitchell to have perjured himself, and implicating Agnew and Connolly in the ITT antitrust fix; 2) helped supervise the Intelligence Evaluation Committee, Nixon's private police, for the White House; 3) supervised the payment of $175,000 to the Watergate conspirators; 4) after the burglary, took incriminating papers from Hunt's White House office and gave them to Gray to destroy; 5) urged Hunt to leave the country after the burglary, at the suggestion of Ehrlichman, according to Colson; 6) met with Donald Segretti† in October 1972, together with Ehrlichman, to plan cover-up of Segretti's espionage-sabotage operations.

Felipe de Diego. CIA *gusano* who partici-

pated in the Watergate burglary but was given
immunity from prosecution to turn state's
evidence. He was also on the Hunt-Liddy
team that burglarized the Fielding office in
Los Angeles, and has indicated through attorneys that if given immunity in that case he
would give information about break-ins at the
Chilean Embassy and at homes of Chilean
diplomats.

John D. Ehrlichman. A college friend of
Haldeman, he began his political career in
1960 as a political espionage agent for Nixon
in that presidential campaign. Working under
Haldeman in that capacity, he spied on Governor Rockefeller in the primaries and on the
Democratic national convention. By the 1968
campaign, he had left direct espionage to
become schedule director for the race against
Hubert Humphrey. After the election victory
he was named to the White House staff and
soon became Nixon's top advisor on domestic
affairs. In that capacity, Ehrlichman: 1) met
with Robert Vesco† in 1972, while the latter
was under SEC investigation, and pledged to
help Vesco take over Intra Bank, in Beirut,
one of the largest in the Middle East, in which
the U. S. government has a major stock interest; 2) ordered the burglary of Brookings
Instiution and the bugging of columnist
Joseph Kraft according to Caulfield† and
Ulasewicz†; 3) initiated for Nixon the setting
up of the Intelligence Evaluation Committee,
the White House secret police; 4) on orders

from Nixon, assigned Liddy and Hunt to
investigate Ellsberg, and, according to David
Young,† ordered the burglary of Dr. Lewis
Fielding, for which he requested the CIA's
help in supplying the necessary materials; 5)
later he tentatively offered the FBI directorship to Judge William Byrne, Jr., while the
latter was presiding over the Ellsberg-
Anthony Russo trial, a clear attempt at
bribery; 6) together with Haldeman, headed
up the White House cover-up of the Watergate burglary, according to Colson, for which
he gave Gray papers of Hunt to destroy;
ordered Dean to "deep six" other secret
White House papers; after the first Watergate
arrests, ordered Hunt to leave the country,
according to Dean; interfered with the FBI
and CIA meeting to discuss the Watergate
investigation; and gave Hunt, through Colson, a promise of executive clemency to keep
quiet; 7) to cover up the My Lai atrocity, he
interviewed several U. S. veterans of the
massacre to get them to deny the facts as
reported by the press; 8) through the FBI, he
had copies of Senator Thomas Eagleton's
confidential health records several weeks before Eagleton made those records public, thus
irreparably harming the McGovern ticket in
1972; 9) through the Treasury Department
brass, he pressured the IRS to hire Caulfield†
and Liddy† to head up an expanded IRS
program to crack down on radical opponents
of Nixon. In 1972, IRS conducted audits on
1,025 such organizations and 4,300 on in-

dividuals; 10) according to Kleindienst,† evidenced interest in executive clemency for convicted Watergaters; 11) said by Kalmbach† to have given okay to hush money payoffs to jailed burglars. Himself accused of burglary, blackmail, hush money payoffs, illegal surveillence, punative tax audits and related crimes, Ehrlichman, a teetotaling Christian Scientist, warned Congress of the dangerous sin of inebriation within its ranks. An obvious hatchetman for Nixon, one colleague says of his efficiency: "He leaves no more blood on the floor than he has to." Facing several possible grand jury indictments, Ehrlichman is now left hanging, to twist slowly, slowly, in the wind.

Pablo Manuel Fernandez. Accompanied the Barker team to Washington to assault Dr. Ellsberg while he spoke at antiwar rally. While working for the FBI and the Miami police he infiltrated the VVAW and attempted to sell weapons to two of what became known as the Gainesville (Fla.) Eight, Vietnam veterans accused of plotting violence against the Republican national convention. Fernandez had also been asked by Martinez to spy on McGovern headquarters in Miami. He is another *gusano* and CIA operative.

Angel Ferrer. President of "Ex-Combatientes Cubanos de Fort Jackson," a group of 800 *gusanos* with military training at Fort Jackson, South Carolina, many of whom participated in the Bay of Pigs invasion. Ferrer has personal ties to Virgilio Gonzalez† and Eugenio Martinez,† two of the convicted Watergate burglars, and was himself a guest at the Watergate Hotel the evening of the raid on Democratic party headquarters.

Frank Fitzsimmons. Hand-picked by Jimmy Hoffa to head up the Teamsters' union while Hoffa was in prison, Fitzsimmons became Nixon's closest ally inside the labor movement and also personal friends with Nixon, Mitchell and Kleindienst. As vice-chairman of "Democrats for Nixon," under Connolly, Fitzsimmons' role was to neutralize and win over anti-Nixon sentiment within trade unions. After the election he joined with the growers' associations in California to try to eliminate the more militant United Farmworkers. Fitzsimmons has a history of collaboration with more than just Presidents and employers' associations against working people: he has been working with the Mafia to loot Teamsters' pension funds, and is now under federal investigation for bankrolling with Teamster money at least four Mafia operations, including Las Vegas casinos, a series of Orange County (Calif.) real estate deals totaling about $40 million, a country club in San Diego used for rest and rehabilitation by organized crime, and a possible billion-dollar-a-year health plan business. (The San Diego country club under investigation is the La Costa, the meeting place where

Haldeman,† Ehrlichman, Dean and White
House aide Richard Moore war-gamed contingency plans to neutralize the impending
Senate investigation. Among the methods
agreed upon were continuing payoffs to keep
Watergate defendants quiet, and smear
campaigns against members of the Senate
committee.) Because of his friendship with
and political support of the Nixon Administration, the Attorney General decided not to
prosecute his son, Richard Fitzsimmons, on a
credit card fraud charge, similar to that which
sent Mafioso Bill Bonnano to prison. Attorney General Kleindienst† stopped an FBI
wiretap (this one legal) seeking evidence to
prosecute in the Teamster-Mafia dealings. In
March 1973 Fitzsimmons was presented with
a Israel Silver Anniversary award at a Washington dinner for Israel Bonds, at which three
cabinet members, including Kleindienst,
were present, together with a large repre-
sentation from the crime syndicate.

Leonard Garment. Chief counsel to the President since May 1973, replacing Dean. Another former partner in the Nixon-Mitchell
New York law firm, Garment was recruited
into the White House by Mitchell. Considered by the mass media as the White
House liberal, he has indeed been a sheep in
sheep's clothing, doing the wolf's work. He
was Nixon's chief negotiator with the American Indian Movement during the takeover of
the Bureau of Indian Affairs building in

Washington and the insurgency at Wounded Knee, where he drew up the government agreements ending hostilities, only to disregard the agreements later. Also for Nixon, he rejected the plea of 50,000 Kent State students and their supporters for a federal grand jury investigation into the National Guard murder of four students in 1970.

Howard Berry Godfrey. An FBI informer, Godfrey organized and financed the Secret Army Organization, a neofascist paramilitary group, as a split-off from the Minutemen. While on FBI payroll, he participated in at least one shooting and several burglaries and firebombings of homes and offices of radicals in the San Diego, California, area. Godfrey met with Donald Segretti† to plan kidnappings of demonstrators at the Republican convention.

Virgilio Gonzales. Another CIA *gusano* and Bay of Pigs veteran, he was convicted as one of the Watergate burglars. He also participated in the physical attack on Dr. Ellsberg near the Capitol building.

George K. Gordon. Working under Kenneth Reitz† he organized students on campuses to spy on antiwar Democrats. Gordon recently left his Department of Interior post.

L. Patrick Gray III. A former Navy officer, he first met Nixon in 1947, when the young Congressman was starting to make headlines with the Alger Hiss investigation. When

Nixon became Vice-President, Gray became
one of his military advisors. During Nixon's
first Presidential term, Gray became an ad-
ministrator in the Department of Health, Education and Welfare, and in 1970, at the urging
of Robert Mardian,† he became Assistant
Attorney General in charge of the civil division. When Kleindienst became Attorney
General, Gray was made his deputy. When
J. Edgar Hoover passed on to the Great Dossier Room in the Sky, Gray was nominated by
Nixon to be his successor as FBI director. As
acting director, he said that the object of the
criminal justice system should be "the protection of society, not just the protection of
the rights of the acused." Gray now stands
accused of: 1) Under orders from Ehrlichman,
destroying Hunt's incriminating documents
passed on to him by Dean; 2) intervening
with the CIA on behalf of the White House to
get the CIA to build an excuse (covert CIA
operations in Mexico) to hinder the Watergate investigation; 3) turning over to Ehrlichman the confidential psychiatric records
of Senator Thomas Eagleton; 4) helping,
through Mardian, plan provocations at the
Democratic and Republican conventions
with *agents provocateurs*. Now facing indictment on charges of obstruction of justice,
Gray has told friends that he has comtem-
plated suicide.

William E. Griffin Abplanalp's† lawyer and
business partner, Griffin purchased two

waterfront lots at Key Biscayne from Nixon, paying the President $150,000; Nixon had originally paid only $53,000 for the lots. Together with Abplanalp, Griffin is a major stockholder in a new Yonkers (N. Y.) federal bank which received its charter in 1971, one of only four to do so in New York State. Other stockholders include Charles Emmett Lucy, a law partner of Murray Chotiner†; and Martin Higgins, who committed suicide in 1973, an act with no apparent link to Watergate.

Nelson Gross. Leader of the Republican party in New Jersey, he first came into national prominence by splitting the N. J. GOP in 1968 and delivering its vote to Richard Nixon. He served as head of the Nixon reelection campaign in 1972, and is now under indictment for masterminding an income tax fraud involving the financing of the 1969 gubernatorial race in his home state.

Edward J. Gurney. Right-wing Republican Senator from Florida and the main Nixon apologist on the Ervin committee investigating Watergate. His administrative assistant, Mike Carr, was a CRP functionary in Florida in 1972 and helped organize entrapment for prosecution of the Vietnam Veterans Against the War. Gurney received over $20,000 in cash gifts from Chotiner,† Charles Morin,† and Bebe Rebozo† a week after the Ervin committee began conducting public hearings. The money, Gurney argued, was a contribution to his re-election campaign, more than a year away. Larry Williams, a voluntary staff member in Gurney's office demanded $5,000 in the last election campaign from a Florida contractor in return for federal approval of two apartment projects costing $6 million.

General Alexander H. Haig, Jr. A member of Gen. Douglas MacArthur's staff during the Korean War prior to MacArthur's removal for advocating bombing China, Haig was well trained for his later assignments in the Indochina war. Very early on he became special assistant to Defense Secretary Robert Mac Namara, and later was the top aide to Henry Kissinger† when the latter presided over strategic decisions like the massive bombing raids of civilian populations. Politically loyal to Richard Nixon, Haig was a key prosecution witness against Daniel Ellsberg in the Pentagon Papers case. In May 1973, Nixon appointed him to replace Haldeman as his chief of staff, at a time when he was vice chief of staff of the U. S. Army. Until August 1973 he served in both positions, in violation of the U. S. Code. He is now being sued by former National Security Council aide Morton Halperin for ordering an illegal wiretapping of Halperin's home.

H. R. Haldeman. The grandson of the founder of the Better American Foundation, an early anti-communist organization, Haldeman first became a Better American as director of the west coast office of the J. Walter Thompson advertising agency, where he handled the

Sani-Flush, Black Flag insecticide, Griffin
shoe polish and 7-Up accounts. He went into
politics as the advance man for Nixon's
Vice-Presidential campaign in 1956 and re-
peated the service in the 1960 presidential
race. He had advanced to the position of
campaign manager by the 1962 California
gubernatorial campaign, during which he and
Nixon were found guilty by California courts
of campaign improprieties (the placement of
fraudulent advertisements in newspapers).
As Nixon's White House chief of staff through
April 1973, Haldeman controlled all access to
the President and all decisions flowing from
the White House. As "Lord High Execution-
or" for the White House, he authorized "any
means, legal or illegal," to keep antiwar demonstrators out of Nixon's sight, according to
Dean. In this capacity he: 1) ordered an FBI
investigation into the background of CBS
correspondent Daniel Schorr, a White House
critic, under the "cover" of considering
Schorr for a White House post; he also ordered a tax audit of *Newsday* reporter Robert
Greene after Greene wrote an investigative
series on the shady business dealings and
relationships to reorganized crime of Bebe
Rebozo;† and he 2) told an NBC "Today"
television audience, regarding antiwar critics
of Nixon: "The only conclusion you can draw
is that the critics now are consciously aiding
and abetting the enemy of the United States,"
a charge—never retracted—of treason against
75 percent of the citizenry; 3) personally

pulled the strings that opened the prison
doors for Jimmy Hoffa; 4) hired Chapin,†
Gordon Strachan† and his own protege Ronald Ziegler† onto his personal White House
staff; 5) placed another protege, Jeb Magruder,† in the number two position in CRP; 6)
was one of five persons authorized to dis-
tribute secret and illegal campaign funds; 7)
kept $350,000 in cash in the White House
safe for use in clandestine activities; 8) controlled the Donald Segretti† spy operation
until February 1972 when it was turned over
to Liddy and Hunt; 9) approved of Colson's†
phoney advertisements supporting the Haiphong mining; 10) according to Dean, was
among those in charge of the Watergate conspiracy funds and selected Democratic party
chairman Larry O'Brian as a subject for illegal
wiretaps; received Watergate wiretap logs
previous to the June 17, 1972, arrests; after
the Democratic headquarters burglary, ordered all documents destroyed which linked
the burglary to the White House; 11) requested the CIA, at "the President's wish," to
help halt the investigation of the Watergate
crimes; 12) tried to enlist North Carolina
Republican leaders to dig up incriminating
evidence of indiscretions in the past of Senator Sam Ervin, the chief congressional investigator, so as to discredit Ervin before the
Senate hearings began; 13) urged plants of
stories that antiwar protestests were financed
by foreign "communist" funds linked to Mc-

Govern; 14) supervised the expenditures of $10 million of government funds for repairs of the Nixon,† Abplanalp† and Rebozo† properties. Haldeman has no known hobbies other than taking home movies of Richard Nixon. He and Ehrlichman are considered by Nixon to be "two of the finest public servants" the President has known.

Paul Hall. President of the Seafarer's International Union, Hall is believed to possibly be heir apparent to George Meany as AFL-CIO president. His SIU donated $100,000 to the CRP. The money was borrowed from New York's Chemical Bank, whose chairman is Harold H. Helms, co-chairman of the Nixon finance committee. The SIU contribution came in return for the Justice Department dropping its efforts to prosecute SIU for illegal contributions to earlier campaigns.

Richard Helms. Now U. S. Ambassador to Iran, Helms was CIA director from 1965 to early 1973. As CIA chief he ordered a personality file prepared on Daniel Ellsberg, the first one on a U. S. civilian the CIA ever made. Later he agreed to supply Hunt and Liddy with the materials used in the bag job of Dr. Fielding's office in California. White House secret documents on the construction of a Presidential private police show that Helms helped formulate an active CIA role in domestic affairs in violation of the law. Having been pressured by Ehrlichman and Haldeman to provide a CIA cover for the Watergate job, Helms has said he believes Nixon ordered the cover-up.

Lawrence Higby. Known in the White House as "Little H" (Haldeman was "Big H") or "Haldeman's Haldeman," Higby told Dean that Haldeman wanted 24-hour surveillance of Senator Edward Kennedy. Higby also initiated attempts to dig up discrediting information on Senators Lowell Weicker and Sam Ervin for purposes of lessening the impact of the Senate hearings on Watergate. Higby remains on the White House staff.

Howard Hughes. The reclusive multibillionaire has been a financial contributor to Nixon campaigns since at least 1952, when he helped fill the famous slush fund which resulted in the "Checkers" confession over national television. Hughes' public relations work is handled by Robert Mullen† and Co., of which Hunt was vice-president. And, through Hunt and Liddy, Hughes gave the CRP a *blank* check. James McCord† testified that there was a plan by Hunt and Liddy to burglarize the offices of a Las Vegas newspaper publisher who is involved in a lawsuit against Hughes, after which a Hughes plane was waiting nearby to take the burglars to a Central American country. *Newsweek* has reported that Hughes is a business partner with Robert Vesco† in Central America. With his longtime ties to Las Vegas gambling interests, Hughes has kept his relations with

Nixon indirect. His attorney is the brother of
Archibald Cox, special prosecutor in the
Watergate case.

E. Howard Hunt. For 20 years a CIA agent,
Hunt's stations have included Paris, Vienna,
Mexico City, Tokyo and Montevideo. He was
a key operative in putting together the CIA-
United Fruit Co. overthrow of the legally
elected Arbenz government in Guatamala in
1954. Later he became personal assistant to
CIA director Allen Dulles and supervised the
mercenary Cuban exiles during the Bay of
Pigs invasion, at which time he urged the
assassination of Fidel Castro, under the invasion's "action officer," Richard Nixon. During
his Paris CIA days he came in contact with
Robert Mullen who was working with the
CIA, and later Hunt became vice-president of
Robert Mullen and Co., which does public
relations in Washington for Howard Hughes
and for the Republican party. Hunt's other
business interests include real estate, where
he has had separate partnerships with Barker,† Rebozo,† and Nicaragua dictator Anas-
tasio Somoza, the latter another friend of
Hughes. Hunt was himself a $100-a-day con-
tractor to CRP, besides services rendered.
Brought into the White House in 1971 by
Charles Colson, who was to supervise his
activities as a key operative of the Nixon
secret police, Hunt had a busy 14 months at
the service of the President. In that time, he:
1) forged cables purporting to be from John F.

Kennedy, implicating the late President in the murder of Saigon dictator Diem; 2) compiled a dossier on the personal life of Senator Edward Kennedy; 3) under the supervision of Attorney General John Mitchell,† supervised the illegal wiretapping of *New York Times* correspondents; 4) planned a bag job on the offices of the Las Vegas *Sun*; 5) headed a White House assassination team in Mexico where he was to be the hit man on a contract on Panamanian President Omar Torrijos, because of the latter's opposition to U. S. occupation of Panama; 6) together with Liddy, burglarized the offices of Dr. Lewis Fielding; 7) travelled to Denver to quiet ITT lobbyist Dita Beard whose memorandum on the ITT bribery of the Nixon Administration was becoming embarrassing. He and Liddy are also being investigated for a series of other burglary and breaking-and-entering jobs— against the NAACP Legal Defense Fund in New York and the Chilean Embassy in Washington, among them. As he and Liddy made their various undercover trips around the country, they used the cover of being representatives of the Howard Hughes Tool Company. Hunt was arrested and convicted for his participation in the Watergate burglary. He effectively blackmailed the White House, through Ehrlichman, Colson, and Frederick LaRue,† accepting $200,000 and a promise of executive clemency in return for his silence. His wife, Dorothy Hunt, also a former CIA agent and member of the Spanish embassy staff, was killed in a United Air Lines crash near Chicago in late 1972. Her death came soon after she told McCord that she and her husband had enough information to impeach Nixon and after they "threatened to blow the White House out of the water." At the time of her death, Dorothy Hunt was on a financial errand involved with the Watergate cover-up; $10,000 in $100 bills were found on her person at the scene of the crash. The money was in wrapping marked "F. S.," leading investigators to conclude that Frank Sturgis† was either the sender or intended recipient of the money. Her estate and the Hunt children are being cared for by William Buckley, a longtime family friend and the children's godfather. Hunt is himself the godfather of one of the children of Manuel Artime, military leader of the Bay of Pigs invasion, and organizer of the "Miami Watergate Defense Relief Fund," a conduit for Hunt-Kalmbach† funds to keep jailed Watergaters quiet.

Tom C. Huston. National chairman of Young Americans for Freedom in 1965, Huston's historic hero is John C. Calhoun, the Southern theorist of states rights. In 1966 he organized the "World Youth Crusade for Freedom," to counter antiwar sentiment on the nation's college campuses. After serving as an army intelligence officer for a couple of years he was brought into the White House by Haldeman and became a Nixon speechwriter and assistant counsel to Dean. As White

House coordinator of security affairs he was chosen to draft the Nixon plan for a super-secret Presidential police and espionage unit, which included mail surveillance, breaking and entering, illegal wiretapping, monitoring overseas cables and phone calls to and from all U. S. citizens, campus espionage units and provocateurs, and CIA surveillance of U. S. students travelling or living abroad.

Herbert W. Kalmbach. The unofficial head of the exclusive Lincoln Club in Newport Beach, California, a group of millionaires committed to the political fortunes of Richard Nixon, Kalmbach was Nixon's personal attorney for five years until May 1973. He raised $6 million dollars for the 1968 campaign and $9 million in 1972. After the 1968 campaign, he controlled the $1.9 million surplus account, which was used to finance the White House secret police. Kalmbach himself had $600,000 in cash for clandestine activities during the 1972 elections. From this money he paid more than $30,000 to Donald Segretti† for his operations, and paid the expenses and salary for Anthony Ulasewicz.† Other leftover monies from 1968 he placed in control of Haldeman's† brother-in-law. Kalmbach paid the hush money to the Watergate defendants and destroyed all of his own campaign finance records, both federal crimes. His political activities were more than a little gratifying personally: in 1968 he had three other attorneys working for him,

with few major clients. Under the Nixon
Presidency, he has 24 attorneys and 200
important clients, including United Air Lines
(see Chapin,† Hunt†) and the Marriott Corporation, whose vice president is F. Donald
Nixon,† brother of Richard. During the 1972
election campaign, Kalmbach secretly purchased the California direct mail house being
used by George McGovern, sabotaged large
McGovern mail appeals by "losing" them in
the warehouse, and secretly sold the company after the election.

Henry Kissinger. For years the top foreign
policy analyst for the Rockefeller Foundation, Kissinger got the opportunity to put his
ideas into practice as Nixon's chief foreign
policy maker, in which capacity he committed untold war crimes against the peoples of
Indochina. It was he that urged the invasions
of Laos and Cambodia, two neutral countries,
and the massive carpet bombings to terrorize
North Vietnamese civilian populations during Christmas week 1972. (Earlier, in 1969, he
urged similar widespread bombing against
North Korea in response to the downing of a
U. S. spy plane over that country.) After the
details of the Watergate crimes were exposed,
implicating Nixon and his top officials, Kissinger became the first apologist for the cover-up, asking for "compassion" for the criminals. At first believed to be pleading the cause
of others, it has developed that his compassion was not exactly altruistic. He had loaned

one of his top aides, David Young†, to work on the White House police project; he had asked the FBI to place illegal taps on the phones of a number of his assistants; he had himself, according to Mitchell, attended White House sessions planning the Watergate cover-up; he had requested the CIA to make up the personality profile of Daniel Ellsberg; he had ordered the wiretap of Morton Halperin's home, for which he is now being sued; and, according to Colson, he was the one who formulated the idea for the parapolice "plumbers" unit, and tried to run the group through Young.

Herbert Klein. Another Nixon crony for years, dating back to the 1950 smear campaign against Helen Gahagan Douglas. As Nixon's director of communications, he hired Herbert Porter,† Gordon Strachan† and Magruder.† Formerly editor of the San Diego *Union*, Klein's main White House responsibility was to travel the national speech circuits, stumping against his former colleagues of the press. The man who helped draft the Nixon "Checkers" speech, Klein declared that "truth will become the hallmark of the Nixon Administration," and that Nixon would "eliminate any possibility of a credibility gap." He resigned from the White House in May 1973 to become vice president of Metromedia, Inc.

Richard Kleindienst. A protege of Senator Barry Goldwater, Kleindienst was named deputy Attorney General under John Mitchell† during the first Nixon term, and brought John Dean,† a classmate and close friend of Barry Goldwater Jr., into the Department of Justice. Earlier, in the 1968 campaign, he had been Nixon's national campaign director of field operations, under Mitchell. As Mitchell's assistant at the Department of Justice, Kleindienst made arrangements with ITT to drop the government's suit in the matter of the takeover of Hartford Fire Insurance; oversaw the Supreme Court nominations of Harold Carswell and Clement Haynesworth; ordered the illegal arrest of almost 15,000 antiwar demonstrators during May Day 1971; and blocked an investigation of illegal ITT campaign gifts to CRP of $100,000 through its Sheraton Hotels subsidiary. When Mitchell resigned to take over CRP, Kleindienst became Attorney General, a position he kept for just over a year. During that time, he: stopped FBI surveillance of the Teamsters' union after the FBI had begun to strip the cover from a Mafia plan to reap millions of dollars in payoffs from Teamster welfare funds (see Fitzsimmons†); ordered Gray not to testify about Watergate at his own Senate confirmation hearing on his nomination as FBI permanent director; argued before the Senate that the President's executive privilege accrued to any employee of the executive branch, embracing some 2.5 million persons from the President to mail sorters. Kleindienst discussed with Ehrlichman how to

keep Senator Lowell Weicker from embarass-
ing Nixon during the Senate Watergate hearings. Ehrlichman said that Nixon thought
Kleindienst ought to "take a swing" at Weicker during a press conference. Ehrlichman
used the phrase in the figurative sense, of
course, since he used Barker's† *gusano* gang
for literal interpretations. Kleindienst was
accused by Senator Henry Jackson of having
"bypassed normal procedures and safe-
guards" in ordering executive clemency for
New Jersey Mafioso, Angelo DeCarlo, who
has been linked to Agnew crony, Frank Sina-
tra. DeCarlo, having served only 19 months of
a 12-year sentence, was released on grounds
that he had terminal cancer, although he is
now back on his feet at work in his chosen
profession.

Egil Krogh. A former law partner in Ehrlichman's Seattle firm, Krogh also served
with the Agency for International Development in Vietnam. When he came into the
White House he was put in charge of the
Special Action Office for Drug Abuse Prevention, centralizing narcotics control in the
White House under executive order. At the
time Krogh said, regarding opponents of
the centralization, "Anyone who opposes us,
we'll destroy. As a matter of fact, anyone who
doesn't support us, we'll destroy." His assistant at the White House was G. Gordon Liddy.† Under Ehrlichman's instructions, Krogh
supervised the burglary of the office of Dr.

Lewis Fielding, the Ellsberg psychiatrist, employing David Young,† Hunt, and Liddy as his main assistants. He was forced to resign as Undersecretary of Transportation in May 1973, a post he had held only five months; he was appointed the day after the crash of Mrs. Hunt's plane and was placed in charge of the investigation of the crash.

Melvin Laird. Former Republican congressman from Wisconsin, he was Secretary of Defense in Nixon's first term, making him a major war criminal. When Ehrlichman left the White House, Laird took over as Nixon's top domestic advisor. While still Defense Secretary, he pressured the SEC in behalf of Edwin Ball, chairman of the Florida East Coast Railway, to drop charges involving illegal sales of railroad stock. Ball's sister, Mrs. Alfred DuPont, had contributed $100,000 to the Laird Youth Leadership Foundation, an "educational institution" in Laird's home district. After being appointed to the White House upper echelon, Laird argued that "the American agenda of issues and problems and decisions and dreams deserves our attention right now," and that Watergate should not be allowed to distract us. The polemic was made on the occasion of the 25th Anniversary of the National Institution of Dental Research.

Meyer Lansky. Reputed boss of the national crime syndicate. Through ties to former Cuban dictator Fulgencio Batista, Lansky

once controlled the gambling and narcotics
traffic in Cuba. When the Cuban Revolution
took power, he offered $1 million for the
assassination of Fidel Castro. The architect of
organized crime's takeover of "legitimate"
businesses, Lansky has long-time ties to
Nixon friends and financial supporters Howard Hughes,† Bebe Rebozo† and C. Arnholt
Smith,† and indirectly to Nixon. After a period of exile, Lansky has returned to Florida,
where he still controls the syndicate as well
as in Southern California, Nevada, the Bahamas, and other Nixon haunts.

Frederick C. LaRue. A wealthy Mississippian
with interests in oil and real estate, he helped
run Nixon's 1968 campaign in the South. A
close friend of Mississippi's Senator James
Eastland and a heavy contributor to Senator
Barry Goldwater's presidential campaign in
1964, LaRue became the architect of Nixon's
"Southern strategy," to win the racist bloc
vote. LaRue's White House operations were
secret; with no title, no salary, no listing in
the White House personnel directory, he still
had a pass to come and go at the highest
levels of the Nixon power structure. He is an
admitted Watergate conspirator. LaRue had
been Mitchell's righthand man at the CRP
and, together with Robert Mardian,† destroyed all incriminating records in CRP
headquarters, following the Watergate burglary. He had himself received $350,000 in
secret funds from Strachan† and admits using

$250,000 of that to pay the Watergate conspirators for their silence. He also urged Hugh Sloan Jr.† to perjure himself.

Jerris Leonard. He came to the Justice Department originally as Mitchell's assistant in charge of civil rights. Soon he became head of Nixon's multimillion dollar anticrime program, the Law Enforcement Assistance Administration. Now he is under FBI investigation for using his government position for personal gain. It seems that as LEAA chief Leonard spoke to Glenn Turner† about representing Turner legally, at a time Turner was under investigation by his department. Later Leonard left LEAA to become Turner's representative.

G. Gordon Liddy. A former FBI agent and one-time Treasury Department attorney, Liddy came into the White House as a member of its domestic council, headed by Ehrlichman. Liddy worked under Ehrlichman and Krogh as their representative to the Bureau of Narcotics and Dangerous Drugs and rode in a White House chauffered limousine. A longtime narc, Liddy was a house guest of Myles J. Ambrose, director of the Justice Department Office of Drug Abuse and Law Enforcement (DALE) and was introduced to friends by Ambrose as, "One of us, he's one of the good people." (The good people of DALE have received publicity lately for their series of dozens of illegal wiretaps, breakings and enterings, perjuries, coverups and payoffs,

breaking down doors and terrorizing at gun-
point innocent families. At least three innocent persons were shot and killed by DALE
agents during these raides in 1972.) Like
Hunt, Liddy carried a gun on his person
while at the White House and was known as
the gun lobby's man in the Administration. A
member of Nixon's secret police team, he
participated in most of Hunt's† operations,
including the Fielding and Watergate burglaries. He became the lawyer for the Finance
Committee to Re-elect the President (FCRP)
and advised on the laundering of secret cash
contributions. With Magruder,† he originated
Operation Gemstone, the Watergate break-in,
although he had differences with Magruder,
whom he threatened to kill. Liddy had performed other unattractive chores for the
White House and CRP, like whisking ITT
lobbyist Dita Beard out of Washington and
into a Denver hospital; and drafting a CRP
program to recruit a call girl ring for a kiss-
and-tell operation at the Democratic convention. Liddy also developed a CRP plan,
rejected by Magruder and Mitchell as too
costly, for kidnapping radical leaders, abduct-
ing them to Mexico and returning them to the
U. S. after the Republican convention.

William Lietke. President of the Pennzoil
company, Lietke one day stuffed approxi-
mately $700,000 in cash, checks and negoti-
able stock certificates into a suitcase, which a
Pennzoil vice president carried from Houston

to Washington on board a company plane. The money was delivered to CRP headquarters in the middle of the night, with no receipts given nor asked for. Part of this money was used to pay for the Watergate job.

John A. McCone. Former chairman of the government commission which whitewashed the national guard assault on Watts in Los Angeles in 1965, McCone preceded his close friend Richard Helms as CIA director. Since leaving CIA he has become a director of ITT, on whose behalf he has lobbied with the CIA and Nixon Administration. At one point he offered $1 million to Helms and Kissinger for the overthrow of the socialist government of Salvador Allende in Chile. This was a substantial reduction from the $20 million ITT and others gave CIA to prevent an Allende election victory in 1964.

James W. McCord Jr. A 20-year veteran of the CIA who actually began his intelligence career with the FBI, McCord used to be introduced by Allen Dulles as "my top man." At the time he left CIA he was in charge of security for CIA headquarters at Langley, Virginia. When he was arrested during the Watergate burglary he was security chief for both CRP and the Republican party. He was also a lieutenant colonel in the Air Force Reserve, serving with a special 16-man unit in the White House basement called the Office of Emergency Plans and Preparedness. The job of the unit was to study "emergencies, radicals and contingency plans"—what to do in case of national emergency. Mc-Cord's job in the group was to draft a "National Watchlist" as part of a contingency plan, the list to contain "information the censors will look for as they open letters, monitor broadcasts and question travelers." The "Emergency Plans" group of military and intelligence officers recalls the news stories in 1970 that Richard Nixon had ordered a study be made by the Rand Corporation of the possibility of cancelling the 1972 elections. (Rand is the Air Force-sponsored think tank.) Among McCord's activities at CRP, other than Watergate, were to provide a background profile of columnist Jack Anderson, who was embarrassing the White House with his investigations; and to open bank accounts for unreported funds under such names as "Dedicated Friends of a Better America."

Roemer McPhee. General counsel for the Republican national finance committee, he is accused by Dean of "having private discussions with the federal judge" presiding over a $6.4 million civil suit brought by the Democratic party in connection with the Watergate buggings. The judge, Charles R. Richey, said McPhee was a neighbor and a close personal friend, but he could not recall discussing the suit with him, "except maybe a very casual thing like, 'Gee, I wish I didn't have the darn case.'" In the summer of 1972, McPhee met

10 times with John Mitchell,† in what are believed to be efforts to influence Richey.

Neil McReynolds. The public relations official for ITT went to Idaho, the home state of Senator Frank Church, to dig up discrediting information on the Senator, who launched the congressional probe into ITT attempts to overthrow the Chilean government.

Jeb Stuart Magruder. With a background in merchandising cosmetics and women's hosiery, he came into politics as a Goldwater aide in the 1964 presidential race. By 1968 Magruder was Southern California director of the Nixon campaign. After the election victory, he became deputy direction of communications under Herbert Klein† and was named temporary head of CRP when it began and Mitchell was still Attorney General. When Mitchell moved into the CRP, Magruder moved down to the number two spot in the campaign and was generally considered to be Haldeman's man in the operation. He recruited operatives and paid them thousands of dollars to disrupt Democratic primary campaigns. With Liddy he formulated "Operation Gemstone" and he supervised Liddy throughout the Watergate burglary. Magruder was the one who asked Sloan and Porter to perjure themselves about monies given to Liddy, and admits to having himself given perjured evidence 12 times in the Watergate trial and to investigators. For his efforts he

was named Assistant Secretary of Commerce
in a new position created just for him. The
post closed down when he was forced to
resign in April 1973 after the Watergate operation started to break open.

Robert S. Mardian. Heir to a family construction company in Phoenix, Mardian is another Goldwater-Kleindienst protege. Under
Mitchell's leadership, he was Nixon's western states manager during the 1968 campaign,
a post he held for Goldwater in 1964. With
Nixon in the White House, he was brought in
as chief counsel to the Department of Health,
Education and Welfare where he developed
Nixon's southern school and anti-busing
strategies. From HEW, Mardian went into the
Justice Department to become Mitchell's Assistant Attorney General in charge of internal
security, the section built up by the anticom-
munist hysteria at the height of the cold war.
In his new position, he set up the interdepart-
mental intelligence unit, with the CIA, NSA,
and FBI, at the request of Nixon. This served
as the basis for the Intelligence Evaluation
Committee, proposed by Nixon to intercept
mail, tap phones, audit income tax returns,
and for "surreptitious entry," Nixon's words
for breaking and entering. Mardian possessed
at the time an emergency telephone "hot
line" to the President's Oval Office. At the
same time Mardian supervised at the Justice
Department Guy Goodwin, who organized a
series of grand juries to hand down "con-

spiracy" indictments against radicals like the Camden 28, the Harrisburg 7, Seattle 7, Black Panther party, VVAW 8 and others. The FBI, under Mardian's tutelege, infiltrated young radical groups and set into motion provocative acts, thus providing the government with a rationale for crackdowns. This technique of setting many little Reichstag fires[2] reached its peak with FBI infiltration and provocations at the Democratic and Republican conventions, creating a pretext after the fact for the Watergate burglary and related activities. Before Watergate, Mardian took the Kissinger illegal wiretap logs from the FBI and gave them to Ehrlichman. He gave Liddy and Hunt Justice Department files a year before Watergate. During the primary campaigns he gave McCord daily FBI reports on the comings and goings of Democratic candidates. This was another aspect of his coordinating intelligence agencies for the White House. After Watergate, he and LaRue destroyed all incriminating CRP documents.

Eugenio Martinez. Still another *gusano*, he was an active CIA agent at the time of the Watergate burglary, for which he was convicted. He also faces indictment for the burglary of Dr. Fielding. A partner in Barker's real estate office, Martinez is vice president of

[2]The Reichstag, the old German parliament, was destroyed by fire, giving Hitler the pretext to crack down on his democratic opposition, in the first place the Communists. Most historians believe the fire was set by Nazi *agents provocateurs* for just that purpose.

another real estate firm with whom Rebozo
and Nixon have done business. He is another
member of Ex-Combatientes de Fort Jackson,
and a veteran of the Bay of Pigs and the
assault on Dr. Ellsberg at the Capitol building.
Martinez offered Fernandez† $700 a week to
infiltrate and spy on McGovern's Miami
headquarters.

William Mills. A protege of Nixon's Secretary
of Interior, Rogers C. B. Morton, Mills filled
Morton's vacant congressional seat in Maryland. (Another Morton protege, Blagdon
Wharton, is now under indictment for receiving an unreported $50,000 gift from CRP to
increase the announced receipts at an unsuccessful fund-raising testimonial to Spiro
Agnew.   Wharton is vice-president of the
Maryland National Bank whose president,
Tilton Dobbin, was vice-chairman of the ill-
fated Agnew testimonial dinner and who is
now Assistant Secretary of Commerce.) Mills
committed suicide in May 1973 after news
reports that he had received an unreported
$25,000 cash gift from CRP.

John Mitchell. Nixon's former law partner,
closest political advisor, Attorney General,
and campaign manager in both 1968 and
1972, Mitchell was the only original cabinet
member invited to buy a house in the Nixon
compound on Key Biscayne. It was in this
Florida home—owned by a bank controlled
by Rebozo†—that he met with Magruder and

Liddy to approve the Watergate bugging. As Attorney General, Mitchell became Grand Dragon of the law and order klan, leading the advocacy of no-knock laws, wiretapping, stop and frisk practices, preventive detention and a "restructured" Supreme Court. His Attorney General and CRP director posts also led him to: 1) illegally arresting 14,500 demonstrators against the Vietnam war on May Day 1971; 2) collect hundreds of thousands of Teamster dollars from Allen Dorfman† prior to the release of Jimmy Hoffa from prison; 3) accept ITT pledges to aid the CRP in return for favorable Justice Department rulings on the ITT takeover of Hartford Fire; 4) falsely testify at the Senate ITT hearings by claiming he was not working for CRP while serving as Attorney General; 5) improperly press Supreme Court justices William Brennan and Earl Warren to reconsider the Court's ruling limiting the use of wiretapping; 6) with Magruder and Lynn Nofziger,† hire a team of American Nazis to deregister American Independent party voters in California, thus sabotaging the George Wallace campaign, to assure the fascist and the racist vote for Nixon; 7) select the Watergate Democratic headquarters as a site for bugging and burglary; 8) authorize payments to Liddy and Hunt to keep them quiet; 9) suggest the plan to burglarize the office of Las Vegas publisher Hank Greenspun to steal documents on Howard Hughes; 10) obtain the release of Robert Vesco† from a Geneva, Switzerland, jail where he had been arrested for fraudulent business deals; 11) help Vesco in an attempt to gain control of the Intra Bank in Beirut, Lebanon, working through the U. S. Embassy in Beirut for this purpose; 12) accept an illegal gift of $200,000 from Vesco for CRP in exchange for interfering in the SEC investigation of Vesco's illegal dealings. For this last action, Mitchell has been indicted on charges of obstruction of justice, defrauding the government and perjury before a grand jury. At his resignation as Attorney General, he was called by Nixon, "our leader against crime and lawlessness."

Charles H. Morin. Charles Colson's law partner, Morin campaigned with Colson† against John Kerry in Massachusetts. He helped pressure the SEC to drop its investigation of Kerry's opponent's business practices. Morin also proposed to Colson to, with White House help, "lean on" C. Bradford Cook† of the SEC to appoint an SEC counsel who would deal favorably with Morin-Colson clients. (One matter before the SEC was an increase in commission rates, following a $75 million loss by New York Stock Exchange members in the first quarter of 1973. Morin is counsel for 53 NYSE members.)

Robert Mullen. President of Robert Mullen and Co., employers of Bennett and Caddy. Hunt, whom Mullen had met in Paris during his CIA days, was vice president of the company. The firm handles public relations for Howard Hughes and for the Republican party.

Harold S. Nelson. General counsel of Associated Milk Producers, Inc., the Texas-based dairy marketing combine. The dairy interests contributed some $700,000 to CRP in return for which the Agriculture Department, on direction from Nixon, raised federally regulated milk prices, giving the dairy interests an annual increase of $300 million a year.

F. Donald Nixon. The President's brother. He put Vesco in touch with Mitchell to arrange a halt in the SEC investigation of Vesco. Nixon is vice president of the Marriott Corporation, which received in early 1973 a $10 million dollar loan from the Greek junta because of his family connections. Kalmbach† is Marriott's attorney.

F. Donald Nixon, Jr. Nephew of Richard Nixon, he lived for a time in Europe with Gilbert Straub.† Now he lives in Costa Rica with Vesco, whom he serves as a personal aide. He calls Vesco his "best friend."

Edward Nixon. Another brother of Nixon, he arranged for Vesco to give the $200,000 to the CRP. He also serves as a trustee of the Richard M. Nixon Foundation, which is to build the Richard M. Nixon Library in San Clemente on the Abplanalp-Nixon property. The other

foundation trustees are Donald Nixon, Ehrlichman, Haldeman, Mitchell, Kalmbach,
David Eisenhower and Rev. Billy Graham.

Richard M. Nixon. 38th President of the
United States. As a Duke Law School student
in 1936, young Nixon broke into the dean's
office to find out his academic standing. Had
he been caught he might have been expelled;
he wasn't caught. As a young lawyer he ran
for Congress in 1946 against Rep. Jerry Voorhis. The candidate of Southern California
corporate interests, Nixon very early on took
up the call of anti-communism, and used
slander to make his way to the White House
(he once described the Presidency to ABC
television newsman Howard K. Smith as
"the top of the greasy pole"). Voorhis, he im-
plied, was "soft on communism," which in
the temper of the time was read as soft on
treason, espionage and sabotage. As congressman, Nixon was assigned to the House Un-
American Committee, an assignment accepted with relish. He returned with HUAC
to Los Angeles to conduct the anti-
communist investigation into the film industry, hearings which resulted in the infamous
Hollywood Ten jailings. He also began investigating Alger Hiss, who coordinated the administrative work setting up the United Nations, and who was an advisor to Franklin
Roosevelt at Yalta. He used the destruction of
Hiss and of his opponent for Senate, Helen
Gahagan Douglas (to Nixon, "the pink lady")

as credentials for candidacy for Vice President. With long-standing indirect ties to organized crime through Chotiner, Rebozo and Hughes, as well as major corporations, Nixon became the ideal VP candidate. Unfortunately some of his support was exposed at the time by columnist Drew Pearson, mentor and predecessor to Jack Anderson. Threats against Pearson came to no avail, and Nixon went on national television with his "Checkers" speech, admitting a secret campaign slush fund, donated by financial supporters. In 1956, at the end of his first term as Veep, it was revealed that Howard Hughest made a loan to F. Donald Nixon of $205,000 taking as collateral a piece of land worth much less. As Vice President, Nixon became "action officer" and coordinator of the plan to invade Cuba at the Bay of Pigs. Between his long-time relationship with Rebozo and this new position, he developed close working relationships with Cushman,† Hunt† and the entire apparatus that was later used for what has become known as the Watergate conspiracy. Defeated by John Kennedy in his first try for the Presidency, Nixon ran for Governor in California in another campaign marked by slander and fraud. (See Haldeman.†) The year before the gubernatorial election, yet another extraordinary Nixon business deal was revealed. It seems the defeated Presidential candidate bought a lot in a Beverly Hills development that had been financed by a $4 million loan from the Teamsters union. The

Nixon lot had cost the builders $42,000 but Nixon paid only $35,000, although the lot next door sold for $99,000. When Nixon sold his lot two years later, he received $86,000, two and a half times his own purchase price. Defeated in the race for governor, Nixon came to New York to firm up his east coast financial ties in preparation for 1968. He joined John Mitchell's law firm. One of his new clients was Pepsi Cola, whose president is an old friend, Donald Kendall. Nixon traveled around the world for Pepsico and dedicated a bottling plant in Vietnam, which has now become the largest heroin factory in all of southeast Asia. Despite receiving AID funds, not one bottle of Pepsi has been produced in the plant. To this day, Nixon continues to support the Saigon Connection. His crimes against the peoples of Indochina have gained for him the reputation among those peoples as the major living war criminal, as he ordered the deaths of over one million people in his four years of office. At home, he set into motion the presidential secret police, answerable only to the White House, to blackmail, mug, steal, open mail and carry out covert criminal activities against government employees, diplomats, antiwar activists, the Black liberation movement, student groups and others. He ordered the FBI under Hoover to put to work "Operation Inlet," to find "items of an unusual twist" regarding prominent personalities. (One such investigation was the snooping into Ted Kennedy's private life, an investigation carried on through official channels and with private gumshoes. Cartha DeLoache had been Deputy Director of the FBI but left the bureau to become an officer in Pepsico, owned by Nixon backer Donald Kendall. DeLoache was asked by Haldeman to research the travels of Mary Jo Kopechne, the Kennedy assistant who was killed in the Chappaquidick accident. When Watergate broke open, Haldeman demanded that DeLoache "produce" evidence that Nixon's 1968 campaign had been illegally wiretapped, to show that Watergate was "just politics." Haldeman told Kendall on behalf of Nixon that DeLoache would have to be fired if he did not cooperate.) This potential blackmail program may have prompted Ehrlichman to secure the Eagleton psychiatric files. Nixon attempted to impose prior restraint for the first time against *The New York Times* and the Washington *Post* to prevent publication of the Pentagon Papers, a decision that was struck down by his own Supreme Court. He is said by Liddy and Mardian to have given his express approval to the Fielding burglary, and later sought to prevent the release of facts to the court about the bag job. Dean testified before the Senate investigating committee that Krogh told him the Fielding job came "right out of the Oval Office." Later, while the Ellsberg trial was in progress, he personally appeared to offer the FBI directorship to the judge in the case. Magruder has said that Nixon was directly involved in campaign planning up to a month after the Watergate burglary. Dean has said he was "personally aware" of the dairy interests' contribution to CRP and that Nixon worked out the details of the deal in the Oval Office. Dean has also said that Nixon met with George Wallace aboard Air Force One and convinced the Alabama governor to run in the Democratic primaries rather than with the American Independent party, thus sewing up the Wallace vote for Nixon, in return for which the Administration dropped a tax evasion prosecution against Wallace's brother. He spoke with Gray about the Watergate cover-up five days after the burglary, ordered Henry Peterson† not to expose the "plumbers" operation, congratulated Dean for preventing indictments above the original seven arrested and tried, and met with Dean 40 times in the first three months of 1973 to make sure the cover-up was "handled right," according to Dean.

While White House statements on Watergate have been declared "inoperative," audits on Nixon's various estates have also been "inoperative," one right after the other. Original claims of only $39,525 of taxpayers money spent for Nixon homes have now been raised to almost *$10 million, not including the cost of security equipment, guards and heliports*. (See Abplanalp,† Rebozo.†) At Nixon's Berchtesgaden in San Clemente, we paid $125,000 for landscaping. Ten thousand dollars were spent to remove weeds "to eliminate a fire hazard," according to a Secret

Service deputy director. He explained, "There were a lot of weeds." The sprinkling system cost $76,000, and another ten grand went for the removal of shrubbery, purchase of shrubs and fertilizer. Congressman Edward Roybal observes, "Shrubbery seems to play a major part in the protection of the President." Another $1,950 was spent to prune trees; argued the Secret Service spokesman, "If a dead branch had fallen down and injured the President or the First Lady, or one of our people, we'd have been criticized for it." More than a million bucks went for home improvements—a beach cabana, heating system for the swimming pool, furniture for the den, etc.—at Nixon's Key Biscayne home which, like San Clemente, is his personal property. Two flag poles were installed and painted for a mere $2,329 at the request of the military, because "Our Commander-in-Chief needs a flag to salute." Generosity was not limited to taxpayers. An ITT subsidiary, Scott Lawn Products Co., provided Nixon with a free golf course at San Clemente, put in during the time when ITT was pressing for a merger with Hartford Fire Insurance, and when the corporation gave CRP $400,000. (See Kleindienst†).

Lynn Nofziger. Formerly press secretary to Ronald Reagan, Nofziger became director of CRP in California. He paid $10,000 in secret CRP cash funds to the American Nazi party to deregister American Independent party voters, thus cornering the fascist vote in California for Nixon. When the facts came to light in June 1973, Nofziger said, "As far as I'm concerned it was legal, moral, good politics, and I'd do it again."

Robert C. Odle. A one-time White House publicity aide, he became director for administration of CRP. In this position he received undisclosed amounts of cash from Herbert Porter,† with which he organized demonstrations—spontaneous in appearance—in support of Nixon's mining of Haiphong. In May 1973 he was hired by the Agriculture Department as a management consultant.

Glenn Parker. A Nazi sympathizer and member of the National Socialist White Peoples' party. He met with Mitchell, Magruder and Robert Walters† in the Los Angeles Hilton, to discuss hiring Nazis to spike the American Independent party registration drive. Walters and he met with Joseph Tomassi† and offered $5000 for the use of Nazi storm troopers as registrars.

Kenneth Parkinson. Hired by CRP as its lawyer shortly after the Watergate arrests, he became the attorney for Mitchell and Maurice Stans.† According to McCord he arranged for CRP funds to pay for the silence of the burglars; payments were made through Dorothy Hunt.

Henry Peterson. Once an FBI clerk, Peterson became chief of the Organized Crime and

Racketeering section of the Justice Department under Mitchell. When Kleindienst became Attorney General, Peterson became
Deputy Attorney General. After Kleindienst
and Patrick Gray resigned, Peterson was
named prosecutor in the Watergate case and a
potential nominee for FBI Director. But his
own role in the Watergate cover-up is quite
direct. He torpedoed the House Banking and
Currency Committee's investigation into the
Mexican "laundry" operation as early as August 1972. He requested that Gray not investigate the laundering of money nor the activities of Donald Segretti.† He instructed the
Watergate prosecution not to inquire into
personal conversations between Nixon and
Dean. In answer to a McGovern charge in late
1972 that the Justice Department investigation of Watergate was a whitewash, Peterson
responded that the FBI and grand jury investigations had been "among the most exhaus-
tive I have seen in my 25 years as a prosecutor," a telling commentary on justice in the
Justice Department. He killed, at Kleindienst's request, the FBI taps of the Mafia-
Teamster deal. (See Kleindienst.†) Indeed he
has been named by Mitchell as a participant
in White House sessions to plan the Watergate cover-up. He is himself under investigation now for obstruction of justice.

Howard Phillips. Another former chairman
of Young Americans for Freedom, he was
named by Nixon to preside over the demise of

the Office of Economic Opportunity. He turned the poverty program apparatus over to a team of former FBI, CIA, Army intelligence and local police Red Squad agents, to spy on the poor. Phillips was removed as OEO acting director in June 1973 for having illegally held office for 6 months inasmuch as Nixon had failed to submit his nomination to the Senate for confirmation.

Reinaldo Pico. Still another *gusano* and CIA veteran of the Bay of Pigs invasion. He also took part in the physical attack on Dr. Ellsberg at the Capitol.

Herbert L. Porter. Another former member of Klein's White House staff, Porter moved to CRP as scheduling director. At CRP he received $100,000 from Hugh Sloan† with which he recruited and paid dozens of people to disrupt Democratic primary campaigns, and funneled funds to Kenneth Reitz† to pay for campus spy operations. With Magruder he set Liddy into motion developing espionage programs. Porter admits giving perjured evidence to the FBI, the grand jury and the Watergate trial jury.

Charles G. "Bebe" Rebozo. Cuban-American, Rebozo had close ties to Fulgencio Batista, the brutal Cuban dictator to whom he introduced Nixon. (Batista's supporters in the United States now form the core of "Cubans for Nixon" and through them came the Watergate bugging unit.) Rebozo made his own fortune during the World War Two rubber shortage when he set up a black market tire recapping business. In 1963 he started the Key Biscayne Bank, of which he is president and whose first savings account customer was Nixon. In 1968 the bank was a repository of stolen checks, channeled to the bank through organized crime sources. Rebozo has long-standing ties to organized crime through the Lansky syndicate, which had controlled gambling, narcotics and prostitution in pre-revolutionary Cuba. He is a real estate partner with Donald Berg, from whom the Florida "White House" was purchased, and who has been linked to a Lansky associate. Nixon was also a Rebozo partner on one real estate deal, investing some $186,000 in 1962, and selling for twice the price ($372,000) seven years later. Even though he is a multi-millionaire, Rebozo has been able to secure five loans from the federal Small Business Administration, under Nixon. (The chief Miami SBA officer is a stockholder in Rebozo's bank.) One SBA grant was used to build a shopping center leased out to right-wing *gusanos*; another was leased to another Lansky mobster. Rebozo is also a close friend of Abplanalp and a real estate partner with Barker. But Rebozo's closest friend is Richard Nixon: they are next-door neighbors in Key Biscayne and constant weekend companions. Rebozo has his own suite in the White House, and he has given his $100,000 Bethesda (Md.) home as a gift to Julie Nixon Eisenhower. After

Nixon's reelection, Rebozo gave the President a bowling alley, built under the White House North Portico. He also gave a bundle of money to Senator Gurney† after the latter was named to the Senate committee investigating Watergate. Rebozo's banking records, deals and associates are presently undergoing Senate investigation regarding the laundering of money rerouted through Miami from Bahamas gambling casinos.

Kenneth Reitz. Reitz was the chairman of the campaign to defeat Tennessee Senator Albert Gore, a key Senate liberal, in 1970. That campaign was characterized by a massive advertising blitz, falsely accusing Gore of being "against prayer." In 1972, Reitz was youth director of the CRP, with a staff of 120 and a budget of $1 million. The money went for numerous and varied purposes—among them bribing a Muskie courier $1000 a month to turn over key Muskie documents to CRP; paying $450 a month to Theodore Brill, Young Republican chairman at George Washington University, to infiltrate radical groups. After the election, Reitz was named director of the "New Majority Campaign" for the Republican National Committee, a post from which he resigned in April 1973.

Elliot L. Richardson. Undersecretary of State, Secretary of HEW, Secretary of Defense and now Attorney General, Richardson has been a nomad in the Nixon years. Says his lifelong close friend, Charles Colson, "Elliot was a guy I could always count on. I told the President that he's a team player." As a member of the Nixon team, he was outspoken in behalf of the Vietnam atrocity while at State; abandoned the busing program at HEW; and as his last act as Pentagon chief, declared that the bombing of Cambodia would continue even if Congress, the Constitutional body for making war, voted to end the bombing. After urging that illegal act, he moved into the nation's top law enforcement post as Attorney General.

Henry Rothblatt. A few years ago the attorney had successfully defended Colonel Robert Rhealt and five other officers of the U. S. Special Forces on charges that they had murdered a Vietnamese double agent. That trial ended in dismissal of charges when the CIA refused to allow its agents to testify about its operations in Vietnam in conjunction with the Green Berets (see William Colby.†) Now Rothblatt is attorney for Barker, Gonzalez, Martinez and Sturgis.

James Schlessinger. Like his precessor at the Pentagon, Elliott Richardson,† Schlessinger has been a traveling salesman for Nixon's various products. He has been a deputy at the Office of Management and Budget where he oversaw the Defense Department's enormous budget. Then he became chief of the Atomic Energy Commission. From February-April 1973 he was CIA director (his background includes time spent as national security analyst at the Air Force's Rand Corporation) and now is Secretary of Defense. At his confirmation hearing for Pentagon chief, Schlessinger proved himself the right man for the job by: 1) defending the bombing of Cambodia as constitutional and "necessary to obtain a cease-fire"; 2) holding out the possibility of renewed U.S. bombing of North Vietnam; 3) arguing for an increased military budget.

Harry Sears. A close friend of Mitchell and attorney for Robert Vesco, Sears is under indictment with his friend and his client and Maurice Stans† for defrauding the United States government and obstructing justice. Sears is former Republican majority leader in the New Jersey Senate and was chairman of the New Jersey CRP in 1972.

Donald H. Segretti. A classmate of Dwight Chapin† at the University of Southern California, Segretti became a lawyer for the Treasury Department upon graduation. After a period in Vietnam, he went to work for CRP under Chapin's and Hunt's guidance and on the payroll of Kalmbach. Under the name "Donald Simmons," Segretti met with Howard Godfrey† to discuss plans to kidnap demonstrators at the Republican convention. His duties at CRP consisted mainly of running its espionage and sabotage branch. It is estimated his network included at least 20 agents. He organized training sessions in Midwest Republican headquarters, teaching Nixon workers to infiltrate Democratic campaigns where the agents were to urge sabotage against other Democratic campaigns. He has been indicted in Orlando, Florida, on charges of mailing a forged letter on Muskie stationery, accusing Henry Jackson of fathering a daughter out of wedlock and of past arrests as a homosexual, and charging Hubert Humphrey with having an arrest record for drunken driving and soliciting prostitutes. Tens of thousands of copies were sent out to Florida Democrats three days before the state's primary election.

Hugh Sloan, Jr. In 1968 the assistant finance director for the first Nixon-Agnew campaign, Sloan joined the White House staff as an assistant to Chapin. In preparation for the 1972 elections, he became treasurer of the FCRP. Among his indiscretions at the finance committee were: 1) the submission of false reports of campaign receipts and expenditures to the Government Accounting Office; 2) the sending of $350,000 in cash to Haldeman, used for the White House private police; 3) the payment of monies to Porter for Reitz' Youth for Nixon espionage operation; 4) the payment of $235,000 to Liddy for his various illegal operations; 5) the destruction of secret cash records, at the instruction of Stans.† Sloan admits to receiving as much as $2 million in cash in the winter of 1971–2. CRP's admitted total of "cash on hand" by April 1972 was $10.2 million, but Common Cause organization, which has instituted a suit against CRP for a public accounting, has

evidence to show CRP had $22 million in
cash by April 7, 1972. Estimates of total CRP
receipts for the Nixon re-election campaign
range from $60 million to three times that
figure.

George Smathers. Still another "Democrat for
Nixon," Smathers used to be a Senator from
Florida. He is a close friend of both Richard
Nixon and Bebe Rebozo, and is also a Rebozo
business associate in deals with the Meyer
Lansky† syndicate. With Rebozo, Smathers
asked Colson† to influence the United States
Parole Board to release from prison Calvin
Kovens, Jimmy Hoffa's codefendant in the
union pension fraud case, because "he is the
most popular Jew in Dade County, South
Florida" and would influence Jewish voters.
Kovens was released eight days after
Smathers asked Colson to intervene in the
matter. Kovens also gave a secret $25,000
donation to CRP. Smathers has also had dealings with convicted Watergater Frank Stur-
gis† who lost his citizenship in 1960. Smathers prevented Sturgis' deportation and re-
gained his citizenship.

C. Arnholt Smith. Another Nixon crony since
his congressional days, Smith controls the
Barnes-Champ Advertising Agency which
was accused of laundering illegal contributions to Nixon's 1968 campaign. Smith also
owns the San Diego Padres baseball team
which is moving to Washington in 1974. A
$350,000 contributor to CRP, Smith is now

under SEC suit for looting $100 million in assets from his own Westgate-California Corporation, a multimillion dollar conglomerate. He has resigned as chairman of the U. S. National Bank, California's tenth largest, with $1 billion in assets. The resignation came one week before the federal Comptroller of the Currency moved against the bank for making illegal loans to Smith's other financial enterprises. He is also under Internal Revenue Service investigation for criminal fraud. The IRS has assessed Smith $22.9 million in back taxes and interest.

Maurice H. Stans. Director of the Bureau of the Budget under Eisenhower, Stans has been a chief Nixon fund-raiser since the latter's first White House days. With Nixon as President, Stans became Secretary of Commerce, but left that post in early 1972 to head up CRP's finance committee. In his farewell speech at the Commerce Department he allowed as how Black people wouldn't have so many problems if they would only read Horatio Alger. Stan's favorite hobby is going on African safaris. On one such hunting visit he made a film of the safari, referring to the porters as "boys." Even the USIA African director called the flick "an Amos and Andy show" and withdrew it from circulation. Stan's fund-raising techniques are apparently more successful than his filmmaking: by his own count, he personally raised $40–50 million for CRP, including $6 million in unre-

ported funds in the two days before the April
deadline. Some of his methods included de-
manding and receiving from defense contractors and munitions makers one percent of
their profits from the government. As Secretary of Commerce he had built up a sheaf of
corporate IOUs by diluting pollution controls, urging import quotas and less stringent
consumer protection standards. Once at CRP
he picked up those IOUs by collecting contribution quotas from executives of U. S.
Steel, American Motors and other monopolies. At CRP he kept from $800,000 to $1.3
million in cash in his safe. The Watergate
burglary was in part paid for by some of these
funds. A week after the Watergate arrests,
Mitchell and Magruder briefed Stans on the
entire affair, and the next day he directed
Sloan to destroy records of millions of dollars
received in cash gifts. Before the Ervin Senate
committee, Stans claimed that he never knew
at any time how the tens of millions of dollars
he raised were spent. The former budget
director of the United States, ex-Secretary of
Commerce, a member of the Certified Public
Accountant's hall of fame, testified that his
destruction of financial records a week after
the Watergate burglary was an "innocent coincidence." He is now under indictment with
Mitchell, Sears and Vesco for perjury before
the grand jury, obstructing justice and defrauding the government.

Gordon C. Strachan. Another classmate of

Chapin at USC, Strachan is one more former member of the Nixon-Mitchell law firm involved in the Watergate conspiracy. He too came to the White House under communications director Herb Klein. When Magruder moved from the White House to CRP as Haldeman's man in the campaign headquarters, Strachan became White House liaison to CRP, reporting from Magruder to Haldeman. Thus all CRP plans for bugging, sabotage and espionage were immediately relayed to Strachan and Haldeman, as were wiretap logs. Strachan had access to the cache of $350,000 in Haldeman's safe, and it was Strachan (according to Dean) who destroyed the Operation Gemstone wiretap logs in Haldeman's office. Strachan and Chapin together directed Segretti's work for Haldeman until February 1972, when the operation came under the direction of Hunt and Liddy. After Nixon was re-elected, Strachan was appointed general counsel of the United States Information Agency, a post from which he resigned in April 1973.

Gilbert R. J. Straub. The former director of European services for International Controls Corporation, under Vesco.† A close friend of F. Donald Nixon† and Edward Nixon,† Straub lived for a time in Germany with F. Donald Nixon, Jr.† Straub introduced Nixon Jr. to Vesco. He also set up the Ehrlichman-Vesco deal to take over Intra Bank in Lebanon (See Ehrlichman†).

Frank A. Sturgis. The overseer of Cuban gambling operations before they were outlawed by the Revolution, Sturgis came to Miami shortly afterward. A CIA mercenary at the Bay of Pigs, he was questioned by the FBI after the assassination of John F. Kennedy because of his *gusano* activities as quartermaster of the exile community's gun and explosives supply. A lieutenant in the Civil Air Patrol Reserve, Sturgis also organized the "Cubans for Nixon" demonstration in Miami in 1972. He was one of the participants in the physical attack on Dr. Ellsberg at the Capitol building, and was convicted as a burglar at the Watergate.

William C. Sullivan. A former assistant director of the FBI, Sullivan was forced to retire in 1971 by J. Edgar Hoover. Sullivan claimed Hoover was growing senile and accused the director of blackmailing congressmen, Mitchell and others in order to keep his position. After Hoover vetoed Nixon's secret police plan *only because Nixon would not put his own signature on the plan*, Sullivan turned FBI files (including the Fielding burglary file) over to Mardian† at Mitchell's request. The files ended up in Ehrlichman's safe. Sullivan is being sued, together with Haig† and Kissinger,† by Morton Halperin for placing illegal wiretaps on his phone. Sullivan is now the Justice Department's director of the Office of National Narcotics Intelligence (see Krogh†).

Joseph Tomassi. The "fuhrer" of the Southern California Nazi party, Tomassi operates out of a swastika-decorated frame house in El Monte, California. He sent 20 of his storm troopers door to door to try to eliminate American Independent party registration, so as to capture the fascist vote entirely for Nixon. Tommassi also received Teamster funds to go "stir things up" against the United Farmworkers in the fields. (See Fitzsimmons.†)

Glen W. Turner. Financial supporter of Nixon, patron of Captain Ernest Medina who led the My Lai massacre (Turner put up his legal fees and offered him a job after acquittal; see Bailey†), and political booster of Lieutenant William Calley, found guilty of murdering women and children at My Lai. Turner is president of Glen W. Turner Enterprises and Dare-to-be-Great, Inc., and is under indictment with Bailey on 28 counts of conspiracy and mail fraud.

Anthony T. Ulasewicz. For 21 years an intelligence agent with the New York police department's Red Squad (BOSS), he was hired by Ehrlichman in a clandestine meeting at LaGuardia Airport and placed on a secret payroll by Kalmbach. As a White House para-policeman, he coordinated with Caulfield† the break-in of Brookings Institution; prepared background intelligence with Hunt on Ted Kennedy's Chappaquiddick accident;

placed the illegal tap on columnist Joseph Kraft's phone; and, on behalf of Caulfield and the White House, served as intermediary with McCord to pressure the latter to cop a plea in return for executive clemency. Other Ulasewicz operations for the White House included investigations of television-caberet performers Tommy and Dick Smothers, and prize-winning filmmaker Emile De Antonio, all critics of Nixon; and the hiring of handsome men to try to seduce girlfriends of the late Mary Kopechne, in an attempt to photograph and blackmail the friends in a campaign against Ted Kennedy.

Robert L. Vesco. The former chairman of the board of International Controls Corporation, Vesco came under civil suit for stealing $224 million in cash and securities from mutual funds. His $200,000 cash gift to CRP, arranged with the President's brother, Edward Nixon, in return for quashing the SEC investigation, has resulted in indictments against Vesco (and Mitchell, Sears and Stans) for fraud, conspiracy and obstructing justice. With his friend and aide F. Donald Nixon, Jr., nephew of Richard M., he has gone to Costa Rica to escape trial. He has invested $2.15 million in the San Cristobal holding company, owned by Costa Rican president Jose Figueres. Vesco was introduced to Figueres by ex-Cuban dictator Batista's former foreign minister, Alberto Inocente Alvarez, now a political and financial power in Costa Rica.

(A new investment firm, InterAmerican Capital, first headed by Alvarez and then by Figueres' son Marti, was the recipient of 60 million Vesco dollars.) Figueres, a leading Latin supporter of Cuban counterrevolutionaries, has seen his personal bank account in New York grow by $350,000 since Vesco arrived in his country. In return, Vesco is allowed to travel on a Costa Rican passport and has tentatively set up an "international financial zone" to which Costa Rican laws wouldn't apply. He has a similar though not so elaborate setup in the Bahamas to whose president, Lyndon Pindling, he has loaned $200,000. The Bahamas, another watering hole of Richard Nixon and his benefactor Robert Abplanalp, is also the home port now of Meyer Lansky's syndicated crime operations since the Cuban revolution came to power. Another Vesco beneficiary is James Roosevelt, still another vice chairman of "Democrats for Nixon," who received $150,000 from the fugitive millionaire.

Robert Walters. An Orange County (Calif.) advertising executive and former George Wallace aide, Walters ran the American Independent party re-registration drive (see Parker,† Tomassi†). He met with Mitchell and Magruder to discuss the use of Nazis to sabotage the AIP and capture the ultra-right vote for Nixon.

Lieutenant General Vernon A. Walters. A military advisor to Nixon when he was Vice

President, he traveled with Nixon during the latter's disastrous Latin American trip. He is now deputy director of the CIA, and met with Dean, Haldeman, Ehrlichman and Gray to discuss the possibility of CIA providing the cover for Watergate. As per "the President's wish," Walters followed Haldeman's suggestion to try to get Gray to call off the FBI investigation of the Watergate burglary. Ehrlichman told Dean that Walters was a "good friend" of the White House and was put into the CIA in order that the White House "have some influence over the agency." Among numerous CIA violations of its mandate which prevents it from domestic U. S. activities, it has (since Walters has been deputy director) trained New York city policemen in the same Red Squad that produced Caulfield† and Ulasewicz.†

John J. Wilson. Chairman of the National Bank of Washington, he is attorney for Haldeman and Ehrlichman and held two conferences with Nixon to discuss the case. Present and former Wilson clients include the United States steel industry, the National Rifle Association, Senator Barry Goldwater; and Interhandel, the Swiss-based chemical corporation owned by the General Aniline and Film Corporation, a front for I. G. Farben which supplied the gas for the Nazi extermination chambers. Wilson demonstrated the racism that prevails throughout the Watergate conspiracy with his characterization, on national television, of Senator Daniel Inouye as "that little jap."

David Young. A top Kissinger aide at the National Security Council, he was loaned by Kissinger to Ehrlichman to work with the "plumbers." Under Ehrlichman, Young supervised Hunt. He arranged with the State Department to let Hunt have access to 240 cables between Washington and Saigon so that Hunt could forge the Kennedy cables. Young also arranged, for Ehrlichman and Kissinger, for the CIA to prepare the Ellsberg personality profile. Together with Krogh,† Young organized the Fielding burglary for Ehrlichman. Young resigned from the National Security Council in May 1973.

Ronald L. Ziegler. As a young man, Ziegler worked driving the Jungle Cruise Boat at Disneyland. After graduation from college, he went to work for Haldeman at J. Walter Thompson agency, where he handled the Disneyland account. With these apparently appropriate and sufficient credentials, Ziegler became, at age 29, press secretary to President Richard Nixon. His press conferences have been compared to the "Five O'Clock Follies," a daily Saigon ritual of lies and pretensions put on by the military for the press corps. After 10 months of denials of White House connections to the Watergate burglary, and characterizing the press investigation of the scandal as "character assassinations," he told the press that his statements of the last year

were now "inoperative." Ronald L. Ziegler
has been kicked upstairs to occupy Klein's
old position, taking him out of the public eye,
ear and nose.